The AA POCKETGuide
KRAKOW

Krakow: Reg

⭐ Best place

◾ Featured sight

The Old Town and Wawel 50–80   Beyond the Planty 93–103

D1355114

Original text by Renata Rubnikowicz
Verified by Mark Baker

© AA Media Limited 2010. First published 2009

ISBN: 978-0-7495-6415-5

Published by AA Publishing, a trading name of AA Media Limited, whose registered office is Fanum House, Basing View, Basingstoke, Hampshire RG21 4EA. Registered number 06112600.

Colour separation: AA Digital Department
Printed and bound in Italy by Printer Trento S.r.l.

Front cover images: (t) AA/J Smith; (b) AA/A Mockford & N Bonetti
Back cover image: AA/A Mockford & N Bonetti

A04167
Maps in this title produced from map data supplied by Global Mapping, Brackley, UK
Copyright © Global Mapping/Daunpol
Transport map © Communicarta, UK

About this book

Symbols are used to denote the following categories:

✚ map reference

✉ address or location

☎ telephone number

🕐 opening times

💷 admission charge

🍴 restaurant or café on premises
    or nearby

Ⓜ nearest underground train station

🚌 nearest bus/tram route

🚉 nearest overground train station

⛴ nearest ferry stop

✈ nearest airport

❓ other practical information

ℹ tourist information office

► indicates the page where you will
    find a fuller description

This book is divided into five sections.

Planning pages 12–25
Before you go; Getting there; Getting
around; Being there

Best places to see pages 26–47
The unmissable highlights of any visit
to Krakow

Exploring pages 48–103
The best places to visit in Krakow,
organized by area

Excursions pages 104–113
Places to visit out of town

Maps pages 117–128
All map references are to the atlas
section. For example, Dom Śląski has
the reference ✚ 119 B7 – indicating the
page number and grid square in which it
is to be found

Contents

PLANNING

BEST PLACES TO SEE

EXPLORING

12 – 25

26 – 47

48 – 103

EXCURSIONS

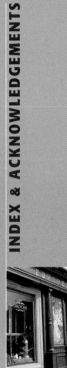

104 – 113

INDEX & ACKNOWLEDGEMENTS

114 – 116

MAPS

117 – 128

Planning

Before you go   14–17

Getting there   18–19

Getting around   19–21

Being there   22–25

Before you go

WHEN TO GO

JAN	FEB	MAR	APR	MAY	JUN	JUL	AUG	SEP	OCT	NOV	DEC
1°C	3°C	8°C	14°C	19°C	22°C	23°C	23°C	19°C	13°C	6°C	2°C
33°F	37°F	46°F	56°F	67°F	71°F	74°F	74°F	65°F	56°F	43°F	36°F

🔵 High season 🔵 Low season

These are the average daily temperatures for each month. May and June are the best times to visit the city – the summer has really begun, but it is not too hot to enjoy the many festivals and the outdoor events associated with them. In summer it can be very hot, the city is extremely busy and thunderstorms can bring rain. July and August are the warmest months, but even in summer you might feel a little cold out of the sunshine.

Going into autumn, September and October can bring golden days with crisp, clear sunny weather, but nights will feel chilly by contrast. Winter can mean dank, murky, very short days, but sometimes there is snow, bringing extra atmosphere to December's Christmas market. The spring months of March and April are the most variable of all.

WHAT YOU NEED

		UK	Germany	USA	Netherlands	Spain
● Required	Ensure your passport is stamped on arrival. A missing stamp can cause problems with Passport Control on your departure.					
○ Suggested						
▲ Not required						
Passport (valid for 6 months)		●	●	●	●	●
Visa (regulations can change – check before journey)		▲	▲	▲	▲	▲
Evidence of financial means to cover stay and departure, which includes onward or return ticket and medical and travel insurance		●	●	●	●	●
Health inoculations (tetanus and polio)		▲	▲	▲	▲	▲
Health documentation (► 15, Health Insurance)		▲	▲	▲	▲	▲
Travel insurance		○	○	○	○	○
Driving licence (national)		●	●	●	●	●
Car insurance certificate		●	●	●	●	●
Car registration document		●	●	●	●	●

WEBSITES

www.krakow.pl
www.krakow-info.com
www.cracow-life.com
www.culture.pl
www.muzeum.krakow.pl

www.karnet.krakow.pl
www.mhk.pl
www.poland.gov.pl
www.poland.travel
www.biurofestiwalowe.pl

TOURIST OFFICES AT HOME

In the UK

Polish National Tourist Office
Westgate House
Westgate
London W5 1YY
☎ 08700 675010
www.poland.travel

In the USA

Polish National Tourist Office
5 Marine View Plaza
Suite 208,
Hoboken, NJ-07030-5722,
☎ 201 420 9910
www.poland.travel

HEALTH INSURANCE

Although EU citizens can use a European Health Insurance Card (EHIC) in an emergency to receive medical or dental treatment, you should not rely on this alone. Whichever country you come from, you should consider buying travel insurance that will give you sufficient medical and emergency cover.

Medical care in Krakow is good and it is becoming a centre for 'medical tourists', who come from other countries for plastic surgery and dental treatment, which is more expensive in their home countries.

TIME DIFFERENCES

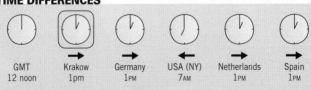

GMT	Krakow	Germany	USA (NY)	Netherlands	Spain
12 noon	1pm	1PM	7AM	1PM	1PM

Krakow is on Central European Time, in winter one hour ahead of GMT, six hours ahead of New York and nine hours ahead of Los Angeles. In summer, clocks go forward one hour.

NATIONAL HOLIDAYS

1 Jan New Year's Day
1 May Labour Day
3 May Constitution Day
Ascension Day 40 days after Easter
Feast of Corpus Christi Thursday after
    Trinity Sunday

15 Aug Feast of the Assumption
1 Nov All Saints' Day
11 Nov Independence Day
25 Dec Christmas Day
26 Dec Boxing Day

Many restaurants and a few of the shops that cater mainly for tourists will not close on public holidays, although banks and businesses will. However, at Christmas and Easter you will find most local people celebrating at home.

WHAT'S ON WHEN

January Carnival season.

February/March Lent: church ceremonies. Processions of hooded Brothers of the Good Death at the Franciscan church every Fri in Lent.

March/April Misteria Paschalia early music festival. Holy Week and Good Friday services. Bach Days music festival.

April All Fools' Day (1 Apr). Easter: Holy Saturday, church blessing of bread and food for families; Easter Sunday, family and church celebrations; Easter Monday, everyone splashes each other with water. Also Emaus festival, fair along ul. Kościuszki to the Rudawa

River; Easter Tuesday, Rękawka festival at Krak's Mound. Easter Beethoven music festival.

May Polish Flag Day (2 May). Constitution Day (3 May). Cracovia Marathon. St Stanislaw procession (Sun after 8 May) from Wawel to Skalka. Corpus Christi: procession with scattering of flower petals. Cracow Screen Festival. Juwenalia student festival. Night of Museums: special events. Lajkonik parade (Thu after Corpus Christi). Film Music Festival. Photography month: exhibitions citywide.

June Krakow Festival. Children's Day (1 Jun). Open Gardens Festival. Pageant to enthrone the cockerel king of the Brotherhood of Riflemen. Wianki Festival (24 Jun): floating wreaths with candles on the Vistula, all-night music and fireworks. Grand Dragon Parade.

July Festivals of Jewish culture, military bands, street theatre, jazz, Carpathian music.

August Folk festival. *Pierogi* food festival.

September Sacrum Profanum festival of contemporary music. Dachshund Parade.

October Month of Encounters with Jewish Culture. Organ Music Days. Krakow Book Fair

November All Saint's Day (1 Nov) and All Soul's Day (2 Nov): everyone visits cemeteries to put flowers and candles on the graves. Independence Day (11 Nov). Krakow's Christmas market opens on Rynek Główny (end Nov–Christmas Eve). Zaduszki jazz festival.

December Feast of Mikolaj (6 Dec), St Nicholas brings children gifts. Christmas cribs on show (morning of first Thu in Dec) in Rynek Główny; the best are exhibited until February at Krzysztofory Palace. Christmas Eve/Christmas Day are family days. Sylwester: New Year's Eve celebrations in the Old Town.

Getting there

BY AIR

Krakow Balice airport

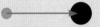

15km (9 miles) to cental Krakow

🚂 30 minutes

🚌 60 minutes

🚕 25 minutes

International flights arrive direct to Krakow's John Paul II International Airport at Balice from many cities in Europe and from North America. It is also well served by low-cost airlines. The airport is expanding and the timetable varies, so it is best to check on the airport website (www. lotnisko-balice.pl). Don't be tempted by low-cost airline claims to fly to Katowice, an industrial and business centre about an hour's drive from Krakow – the transfer is not easy.

You'll see desks for all the main car rental companies in the arrivals hall. If you are visiting Krakow only you are probably better without one.

The best ways to get into the city from the airport are by taxi or train. You can pick up a metered taxi from just outside the international arrivals terminal. The driver will give you a receipt *(paragon)* for the fare if you ask for it. It should take between 20 and 30 minutes to drive to the Old Town, and will cost you 50–60PLN. Alternatively, you can book a taxi with the airport's official company (tel: 9191). If your hotel or hostel offers to send a car to meet you, check the price. It can be a little cheaper than taking a taxi.

Or you can catch a shuttle bus, also from outside the international arrivals hall, for the train from the airport to the main station (Dworzec Główny). Trains leave once every 30 minutes and you can be in the city in under half an hour. Tickets (6PLN) are available on the train or before boarding.

As for local buses, the 292 (departures about every 40 minutes) takes about an hour to get into the city, but one of its many stops may be more convenient for where you are staying. Similarly, the 208 will take you to Nowy Kleparz for 2.60PLN one-way, with a 0.50PLN surcharge if you buy your ticket from the driver rather than from the machine at the bus stop.

BY RAIL

Krakow's Dworzec Główny railway station, just outside the Old Town, is well connected with the rest of Poland and other cities in Europe. Check out www.pkp.com.pl for routes, timetables and ticket information. For express and international trains see www.intercity.com.pl.

BY CAR

The main international motorways through Krakow are the A4 (from Germany through Wrocław, Katowice, Kraków, Tarnów and Rzeszów into the Ukraine) and the A7 from Gdańsk through Warsaw and Kraków to Slovakia. From Krakow it's 295km (183 miles) to Warsaw, 100km (62 miles) to Zakopane and 114km (71 miles) to Częstochowa.

BY BUS

The Regionalny Dworzec Austobusowy bus station is close to the train station (www.rda.krakow.pl). You can also get information from Eurolines, which runs international bus services to Krakow from several cities in Europe. For details of routes, ticket prices and 15- and 30-day European bus travel passes see its website – www.eurolines.com.

Getting around

BY FOOT

Most of what you'll want to see and do in Krakow can be easily reached by walking. The city is fairly flat and most of the sights are grouped close together in the Old Town or Kazimierz.

BUSES AND TRAMS

Krakow's efficient bus and tram service, which includes a night bus network, runs out from the Old Town to the inner city and the farthest suburbs (tel: MPK general 9285, information 9150; www.mpk.krakow. pl). Buy tickets from machines at stops, kiosks near stops or machines on some buses. Machines usually have information in English as well as Polish. Buying a ticket on board means you have to pay an extra 0.50PLN on the basic price of 2.50PLN. Validate your ticket by punching it in one of the orange machines on board and keep it for inspection.

MINIBUSES

You'll see minibuses around the Planty (➤ 93) running from the Old Town to Podgórze or Kazimierz and out to Wieliczka. These are privately run but well regulated. The destination is shown on the front and you pay the driver. Fares are roughly double those on official city buses. Many routes begin at the main railway station, or try the main post office.

TAXIS

Taxi fares are moderate and you'll find taxi ranks just within the Planty at Plac Szczepański, ul. Sienna, ul. Sławkowska and at the junction of ul. Stradomska and ul. Bernardyńska. To call for a taxi, tel: 012 9661 (Barbakan Taxi), 012 9664 (Euro Taxi), 012 9621 (City Taxi) or 012 9191 (Radio Taxi). Use only metered taxis, which are clearly marked.

CITY TOURS AND BEYOND

You can rent a minibus or taxi for all or part of a day. Prices are negotiable but usually fair, and your hotel and hostel will probably be able to recommend a reputable company. There are also regular all-day or half-day tours to popular sights which anyone can join and which might be an option if you are a single traveller.

CAR RENTAL

The Old Town is mostly pedestrianized. The roads in the area just outside the Planty are often one-way, parking is limited, public transport is good, taxis are moderate and most of the sights are within walking distance of each other, so if you are staying in Krakow it's best not to drive. If you're travelling further afield in Poland, you'll find a list of car rental companies on the city website – www.krakow.pl.

DRIVING

- Drive on the right.
- Your vehicle must carry a warning triangle, a fire extinguisher and a first-aid kit.
- You must always drive with the headlights on, night and day.
- Seatbelts must be worn in the front and rear of the vehicle.

- Speed limits are 50kph (31mph) in built-up areas, 90kph (56mph) outside those areas, 100kph (62mph) on A-class roads, 130kph (80mph) on motorways.
- Pedestrians take precedence at traffic lights.
- Beware heavy fines for parking without paying and displaying in controlled zones. Tow trucks are very active in Krakow.
- If you have an accident you must stay on the scene, give first aid to anyone injured, and call an ambulance or doctor and the police.

BOAT TOURS

In summer, between May and October, river cruisers moor at the bend of the Vistula between the Dębnicki and Grunwaldzki bridges. Trips can be anything from half an hour to half a day, which will take you as far as Bielany and Tyniec. Prices are moderate.

VISITORS WITH DISABILITIES

Many of the streets in the Old Town, originally cobbled and uneven, are being renovated to match the smoother, level surfaces of the Rynek Główny, but outside this small area, pavements and roads are often in a bad state of repair and kerbs are high. However, except for Wawel Hill, the Old Town and Kazimierz are fairly flat, though you'll find restaurants, bars and clubs are often in cellars. Galeria Stanczyk information centre for visitors with disabilities, tel: 012 636 8584; open Tue, Thu 11–5.

CYCLING

Cycling is a good way to see the city or get out into the countryside, and prices are reasonable. Eccentric Bike Tours & Rentals (tel: 012 430 2034; www.eccentric.pl) has all sorts or bicycles, or try Cruising Krakow (tel: 012 398 7057; 514 556 017; www.cruisingkrakow.com).

HORSE-DRAWN AND ELECTRIC CARTS

Take a horse and carriage around the Old Town. Prices vary according to the length of the ride, but it is expensive. A more reasonable, if less romantic, option is a Melex tour in one of the electric golf cart-style vehicles, which also wait for passengers in the Rynek Główny. They offer a variety of tours in the Old Town or out to Kazimierz and beyond, and usually feature a recorded commentary in the language of your choice.

Being there

TOURIST OFFICES
City Tourist Information Network
Town Hall Tower, 1 Rynek Główny
☎ 012 433 7310; www.krakow.pl
🕐 Mon–Sun 9–7

International Airport Krakow-Balice
☎ 012 285 5341 🕐 Mon–Sun 10–6

25 ul. Szpitalna
☎ 012 432 0110 🕐 Mon–Sun 9–7

2 ul. św. Jana 2
☎ 012 421 7787 🕐 Mon–Sat 10–6

7 ul. Józefa, Kazimierz
☎ 012 422 0471 🕐 Mon–Sun 10–6

16 os. Słoneczne, Nowa Huta
☎ 012 643 0303 🕐 Tue–Sat 10–2

Wyspiański 2000 Pavilion,
2 Plac Wszystkich Świętych
☎ 012 616 1886 🕐 Mon–Sun 9–7

MONEY
The złoty is the official currency in Poland, usually abbreviated to zł or PLN. You'll find a good choice of bureaux de change, banks and cash machines in Krakow's Old Town and in Kazimierz. Everywhere in Krakow is well served with ATMs.

POSTAL AND INTERNET SERVICES
The city's main post office is at 20 ul. Westerplatte and is open Mon–Fri 7:30am–8:30pm, Sat 8–2. The post office near the railway station at 4 ul. Lubicz has some round-the-clock services, otherwise it's open Mon–Fri 7am–8pm. You can also buy stamps at kiosks. Post boxes

TIPS/GRATUITIES

Yes ✓ No ✗	
Restaurants (if service not included)	✓ 10–15%
Cafés/bars (if service not included)	✓ 10–15%
Taxis (for helpful service)	✓ 10–15%
Porters	✓ 5PLN
Chambermaids	✓ 10PLN a day

are red with the symbol of a yellow horn in a blue disc and the words Poczta Polska.

Koffeina at 23 Rynek Główny is the most central cybercafé (www. cafe.studencki.pl), but there are many others in the Old Town, as well as bars and cafés offering free WiFi. The whole of the Rynek Główny and the centre of Kazimierz have free WiFi and all hostels and most hotels provide internet access. In older hotels, coverage can be patchy, so check when you book.

TELEPHONES

You can buy a local sim card for your mobile telephone at newsagents or kiosks, where you can also buy phone cards. When telephoning within the city you need to use the full Krakow code: 012. Also use the zero before the city code when telephoning other cities in Poland.

International dialling codes
UK: 00 44
Germany: 00 49
USA: 00 1
Netherlands: 00 31
Spain: 00 34

To call Krakow from abroad
From the UK dial: 00 48 12
From the US dial: 011 48 12

Emergency telephone numbers
Any emergency (including ambulance): 999
SOS by mobile/cellphone: 112

Police: 997
Fire: 998

EMBASSIES AND CONSULATES
UK ☎ 012 421 7030;
www.britishembassy.gov.uk
Germany ☎ 012 424 30 00;
www.krakau.diplo.de
USA ☎ 012 424 5183;
www.krakow.usconsulate.gov
Netherlands ☎ 022 559 1200;
www.nlembassy.pl
Spain ☎ 022 622 4250

ELECTRICITY
Like the rest of Europe, Poland uses a 220-volt system and round-pin plugs. Bring an adaptor. US visitors need to make sure their equipment is dual-voltage.

HEALTH AND SAFETY

Drugs For minor illnesses try a pharmacy *(apteka)* first. Many pharmacists speak good English.

Safe water Bottled water is widely available, but Krakow's tap water is safe to drink.

Personal safe Krakow is a safe city with a strong, visible police presence in tourist areas, but as with any city, take care of your bags, money and other valuables, particularly in cafés and bars.

Equally, the police expect visitors to abide by the rules. These include no jaywalking, no littering, no public drunkenness or drinking alcohol on the street. Laws are enforced with on-the-spot fines and drunks are taken to a drying-out clinic overnight and charged for their stay.

OPENING HOURS

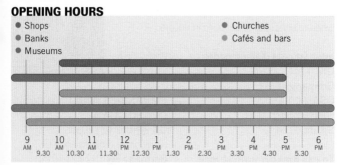

Shops catering for tourists keep longer hours, but most are open Mon–Fri 10–6 or 7, with later opening and earlier closing on Sat (as early as 2 or 3pm). Many but not all shops are open on Sun. There are many small convenience stores in the Old Town and nearby that are open 24 hours daily. Most museums are closed on Mon, otherwise opening hours of museums and tourist attractions vary widely, and many have longer hours in the summer than in the winter. Last entry is half an hour before closing. Banks are open Mon–Fri 8–5, Sat 8–1. Bars, cafés, clubs and restaurants serving a young, party-loving clientele will often open at 9am and stay open until the early hours of the next morning or 'until the last guest leaves' as is traditional in Krakow. Other establishments keep more moderate hours.

LANGUAGE

Krakow is full of people who speak English, but if you attempt to say a few words in Polish you will swiftly make friends. All Polish words are pronounced phonetically and the accent falls on the penultimate syllable.

yes/no	*tak/nie*	excuse me	*przepraszam*
please	*proszę*	help!	*pomocy!*
thank you	*dziękuję*	today	*dzisiaj*
good morning/		tomorrow	*jutro*
good afternoon	*dzień dobry*	yesterday	*wczoraj*
good evening	*dobry wieczór*	how much?	*ile to kosztuje?*
good night	*dobranoc*	open	*otwarty/czynny*
goodbye	*do widzenia*	closed	*zamknięty/nieczynny*
hotel	*hotel*	one/two	*jedna osoba/*
room	*pokój*	people	*dwie osoby*
... single	*... pojedynczy*	reservation	*rezerwacja*
... double	*... dwuosobowy*	rate	*cena*
one/two	*jeden doba (noc)/*	key	*klucz*
nights	*dwie dobe (nocy)*	breakfast	*śniadanie*
bank	*bank*	credit card	*karta kredytowa*
exchange office	*kantor*	foreign exchange	*wymiana walut*
post office	*poczta*	pound sterling	*funt szterling*
cashier	*kasjer/kasjerka*	American dollar	*dolar amerykański*
restaurant	*restauracja*	starter	*przystawka*
café	*kawiarnia*	main course	*główny danie*
menu	*karta/potraw*	dessert	*deser*
drink	*napój*	vegetarian	*wegetariański*
water	*woda*	the bill	*rachunek*
aeroplane	*samolot*	bus	*autobus*
airport	*lotnisko*	bus station	*dworzec autobusowy*
train	*pociąg*	ticket	*bilet*
train station	*dworzec*	... single	*... w jedną stronę/*
platform	*peron*	... return	*... powrotny*

Best places to see

Collegium Maius   28–29

Dom Śląski   30–31

Katedra Wawelska   32–33

Kościół Mariacki   34–35

Muzeum Książąt Czartoryskich   36–37

Muzeum Narodowe w Krakowie   38–39

Pałac Królewski na Wawelu   40–41

Smocza Jama   42–43

Stara Synagoga   44–45

Sukiennice   46–47

Collegium Maius

www.uj.edu.pl/muzeum

There are many places of education in this university city, but this is the one that started it all in medieval times. Now it's a museum holding the college's treasures.

Legend has it that Queen Jadwiga sold her crown jewels to fund the revival of Krakow's university and the construction of this, its main building. King Kazimierz the Great had founded the first Krakow Academy in 1364, but it had lost prestige and power by the time the queen and her consort, King Władysław Jagiellon, came to the throne in 1384. Today, you join a tour to visit the museum, but first take a look at the clock in the courtyard which plays the university song

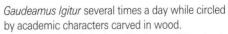

Gaudeamus Igitur several times a day while circled by academic characters carved in wood.

Upstairs, the Library's ceiling is a traditional skyscape, below which hang portraits of eminent scholars. The professors' rooms are furnished with period pieces, while items in the collection span 1,000 years of history. You'll see a charming wooden carving of King Kazimierz from about 1380, the Jagiellonian Globe, which was the first to depict the continent of America, 17th-century Persian carpets and the only surviving drawing by Veit Stoss, the creator of the great altar in St Mary's Church. In the room dedicated to the astronomer Nicholas Copernicus, who studied here from 1491 to 1495 are a collection of astrolabes, including one made in Cordoba in 1054. More recently, another famous student, the film director Andrzej Wajda, donated his Oscar to the university museum. Fun for children is the separate, interactive World of the Senses science exhibition.

➕ 120 D3 ✉ 15 ul. Jagiellońska ☎ 012 422 0549, 012 663 1307 🕐 Main exhibition: 30-min tours Mon–Fri 10–2:20 (last tour), Sat 10–1:20 (last tour); Apr–Oct Thu last tour 17:20. Main exhibition plus scientific and fine arts collections: hour-long tour Mon–Fri only 1pm. Interactive science exhibition: Mon–Sat 9–1:30. Musical clock: daily 9, 11, 1, 3, 5 💰 Main exhibition: inexpensive, free Apr–Sep Tue 3–5:20. Longer tour with scientific and fine arts collections: moderate. Interactive exhibition: inexpensive, Sat free 🍴 U Pęcherza cellar café (€) ❓ Advance booking recommended: main Collegium Maius tours ☎ 012 663 1521; interactive exhibition ☎ 012 663 1319

2 Dom Śląski

www.mhk.pl

Giving a vivid insight into life in Krakow under Nazi rule, this museum includes rooms that were once used as detention and torture cells.

31

This anonymous corner block on ul. Pomorska, initially built in the 1930s to provide accommodation for students from Silesia (Slaśk in Polish), was converted to deadly purpose as the Gestapo headquarters during World War II. Here prisoners were questioned and tortured; thousands died. Across the courtyard from the main museum, the cells have been preserved, their walls still carrying the inscriptions made by some 600 of the prisoners, sometimes written moments before they were killed.

The museum's permanent exhibition, Krakow 1939–56, is small but extremely comprehensive, with a mass of photographs and ephemera, including postcards showing the Nazi flag flying from buildings familiar to any tourist, and Rynek Główny renamed Adolf Hitler Platz. The archbishop of Krakow wrote to the Pope: 'Our situation is very tragic indeed. Deprived of almost all human rights, subject to the cruelty of people who in the majority do not have human feelings, we live in terrible fear and under incessant threat of losing everything in the event of displacement or deportation or of being imprisoned in the so-called concentration camp, from where only a few return alive.' Despite this terror, resistance flourished. The story is easy to follow in the clear English captions.

✚ 119 B7 ✉ 2 ul. Pomorska ☎ 012 633 1414 🕐 Nov–Apr Tue, Thu–Sat and 2nd Sun of month 9–4, Wed 10–5; May–Oct Tue–Sat and 2nd Sun of month 10–5:30 ✋ Inexpensive 🚋 Tram 4, 14, 13, 24 to Plac Inwalidów

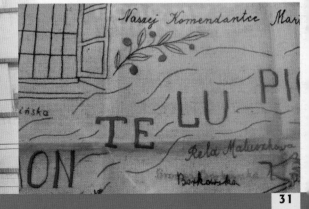

3 Katedra Wawełska

www.wawel.diecezja.pl

The centre of Christianity in Poland, Wawel Cathedral saw the coronations of all its kings and the funerals of many of its rulers and heroes.

Krakow's bishops came to Wawel Hill in about 1000AD and began the first of several churches here. The triple-aisled Gothic cathedral you see today was begun in 1320 and consecrated in 1364, but many of the chapels, such as the Renaissance Zygmunt chapel with its striking gold dome, were added later. As the burial place of St Stanisław, Poland's patron saint, now marked with an opulent silver tomb, the cathedral soon drew pilgrims, and Poland's kings made it a focus of church and state. In the main entrance hang huge bones, once rumoured to be those of the Wawel dragon, but really the remains of prehistoric beasts.

While the royal tombs are in the main cathedral, Poland's kings and queens are buried below in the crypt, as are some of the country's great soldiers, such as Tadeusz Kościuszko, known to Americans as well as Poles, and General Władysław Sikorski, leader of the Polish Government in Exile during World War II. You'll also find the graves of poets such as Adam Mickiewicz, and the altar where Karol Wojtyła, later to be John Paul II, the first Polish pope – said his first Mass. High above the cathedral, in the Zygmunt Tower, hangs the huge 11-tonne, 2m-wide (6.5ft) Zygmunt bell. Polish people believe if you touch it with your left hand you will be lucky in love.

✝ 120 E4 ✉ Wawel 3 ☎ 012 429 3327; www.wawel.diecezja.pl
🕐 Apr–Sep Mon–Sat 9–5, Sun 12:30–5; Oct–Mar Mon–Sat 9–4, Sun 12:30–4. Museum Mon–Sat 9–5, closed Sun and holy days. Last ticket 3:45; last admission 1 hour before closing. Also closed 1 Jan, Maundy Thu, Good Fri, Easter Sat and Sun, 1 Nov, Sun in Advent, 24–25 Dec ✋ Inexpensive
🍴 Cafés on Wawel Hill (€) ❓ For more information, rent an audioguide

Kościół Mariacki

www.mariacki.com

The twin towers of St Mary's Church are the symbol of the city as much as the *hejnał* – the bugle call sounded hourly from the tallest tower.

Begun at the end of the 13th century, this Gothic marvel in red brick was not finished until the beginning of the 15th century, with side chapels and altars added down the centuries, including Renaissance tombs by Italian artists and murals and stained-glass windows from the turn of the 20th century. Inside, the highlight is the magnificent carved lindenwood altar by Veit Stoss, the Master of Nuremburg. Created between 1477 and 1489, it is the largest of its kind in Europe and its 200 gilded and painted figures are so detailed that a 20th-century Krakow professor was able to use it to study medieval skin diseases. As the finest sculptor of his time, Stoss was paid the equivalent of the city's budget for a whole year for his work.

You'll hear the *hejnał* wherever you are in the market square, but you can also climb the tower for a close-up – and good views over the city. The present-day buglers are carrying on a tradition that began in 1241 when a watchman raising the alarm of a Tatar attack on the city was hit in the throat by an arrow. He died, but the city was saved. In his memory, the bugle call is cut off in the middle of the last note. The sound of the *hejnał* is also used as a time-signal on Polish radio.

✚ 120 D4 ✉ 5 Plac Mariacki ☎ 012 422 5518
🕐 Mon–Sat 11:30–6 (High Altar opens at 11:50), Sun 2–6, no visitors during Mass. Tower visits 3 May–Sep Tue, Thu, Sat, 9–11:30, 1–5:30
✋ Inexpensive 🍴 None ❓ Ticket office opposite side door on other side of Plac Mariacki. Tower tickets at base of tower

5 Muzeum Książąt Czartoryskich

www.muzeum-czartoryskich.krakow.pl

www.czartoryski.org

Star of the art collection of the princely Czartoryski family is Da Vinci's *Lady with an Ermine*, but the riches of this gallery also include a fine Rembrandt.

Such is the troubled history of this exceptional collection that it is remarkable how much of it came back to Poland. Princess Izabella Czartoryska began acquiring choice pieces in the late 18th century to preserve some of Poland's heritage, buying Turkish trophies from the siege of Vienna in 1683 and royal treasures looted from Wawel Castle in earlier times. Her son, Prince Adam Jerzy, found the Da Vinci and a Raphael portrait of a young man while travelling in Italy. The romantic Izabella could not resist adding the ashes of El Cid, scraps from the grave of Romeo and Juliet and relics of Abelard and Héloïse, and Petrach and Laura. Later political unrest caused the family to move to Paris with the collection, which by now included Rembrandt's *Landscape with a Good Samaritan*, where it stayed until 1876 when the

city of Krakow, again enjoying more settled times, offered its former arsenal as a museum to house the collection.

In World War II, many of the best pieces were taken to Dresden, but eventually returned. However, during the war, the Nazis running the city took many of the best pieces for Hitler's private collection and incarcerated the curator in a concentration camp where he died. Some 844 items are still missing, including the Raphael portrait. An empty frame hangs on the wall near the Da Vinci, waiting for its return.

➕ 120 C4 ✉ Entrances at 19 ul. św. Jana and 8 ul. Pijarska ☎ 012 422 5566 🕐 Tue–Sat 10–6, Sun 10–4; closed 1 Jan, Easter, 1 and 11 Nov, 24, 25, 31 Dec 🖐 Inexpensive, Sun free

6 Muzeum Narodowe w Krakowie

www.muzeum.krakow.pl

Krakow's National Museum has the largest collection of 20th-century Polish art in the city, a floor of domestic arts and crafts and a gallery of military hardware.

On the top floor of this gallery are all the main names of Krakow's artistic life in the past hundred years. The stars of the Young Poland movement, which took place at the turn of the 20th century – Józef Mehoffer, Stanisław Wyspiański and Jan Matejko – are well represented here, as is the Modernist Stanisław Witkiewicz, known as Witkacy. He was a philosopher, novelist and playwright as well as a visual artist. Independence in 1920 encouraged the arts to flourish and, like Witkacy, artists looked beyond Poland's borders for new ideas. After 1945, the drive towards independence began again, as shown here in pieces by artists such as Tadeusz Kantor.

On the middle floor, the display of decorative arts and crafts stretches back to the early Middle Ages, with lovely silverware, stained glass and embroidery gathered from local churches. You'll also see a selection of 20th-century Polish crafts, showing the different traditional styles of costume and embroidery.

The Weapons and Colours in Poland exhibition on the ground floor also includes exhibits dating back to the Middle Ages, with the focus on the arms, armour and uniforms of the Polish military from the 18th century up to World War II.

➕ 119 D7 ✉ 1 al. 3 Maja ☎ 012 295 5500 🕐 Tue–Sat 10–6, Sun 10–4
✋ Inexpensive, Thu permanent exhibitions free 🍴 Café (€) 🚌 103, 114, 124, 164, 173, 179, 444 to the Cracovia Hotel. Tram 15, 18 to the Cracovia Hotel ❓ A combined ticket gives entry to all three permanent exhibitions for a little more than the price of two

Pałac Królewski na Wawelu

www.wawel.krakow.pl

Wawel Castle, a palace on the hill that overlooks Krakow, was the home of Poland's rulers down through the centuries, and is now restored to give a glimpse of past grandeur.

Although Poland's royal family first came to live on Wawel Hill in the 10th century, the Renaissance palace, with its arcaded, frescoed courtyard, was built in the early 16th century for King Alexander and his successor, Zygmunt the Old. Inside, the walls are hung with Brussels tapestries specially made for Zygmunt II Augustus, and many splendid paintings from the schools of Titian, Raphael and Botticelli. Though it was once the equal of any great palace in Europe, changes in Poland's fortunes meant many of its treasures were looted. At one stage the Austrian army used it as a barracks and stable. During the Nazi occupation of World War II, the tapestries and the 13th-century gold coronation sword – Szczerbiec – were kept safe in Canada.

Many of the grandly decorated State Rooms still have their carved and painted ceilings. The 30 lively wooden heads on the ceiling of the Deputies' Hall are what remains of the original 194. One is gagged, allegedly for telling the king what to do. It's worth visiting the Oriental Art exhibit, which shows the Eastern influences on Polish culture; the Armoury, which has Turkish tents, guns and armour captured by King Jan III Sobieski in the Battle of Vienna in 1683 and a rare Hussar suit of armour with feathered wings, and the Treasury, some of whose hoard of gold and gems goes back to the 2nd century BC.

✚ 120 F4 ✉ Wawel 5 ☎ 012 422 51 55, ext 219
🕐 State Rooms: Apr–Oct Mon 9:30–1, Tue–Fri 9:30–5,
Sat–Sun 11–6; Nov–Mar Tue–Sat 9:30–4, Sun 10–4.
Royal Private Apartments Apr–Oct Tue–Fri 9:30–5,
Sat–Sun 11–6; Nov–Mar Tue–Sat 9:30–4. Crown Treasury
and Armoury: Apr–Oct Tue–Fri 9:30–5, Sat–Sun 11–6;
Nov–Mar Tue–Sat 9:30–4, Sun 10–4; closed 1 and 3 May;
15 Aug Sun hours apply. All exhibits closed 1 Jan, Easter Sat and Sun, 1
and 11 Nov, 24–25 Dec 🖐 All tickets are timed. State Rooms: moderate,
free tickets Mon Apr–Oct, Sun Nov–Mar, includes entry to Oriental Art
exhibit. Royal Private Apartments: moderate. Crown Treasury and Armoury:
moderate, free tickets Sun Nov–Mar 🍴 Wawel Hill cafés (€), shops, ATM
and post office ❓ Two ticket offices (at Bernardyńska Gate and Herbowa or
Coat of Arms Gate); close 1 hour 15 mins before exhibitions. Last admission
1 hour before closing. The arcaded courtyard closes 30 mins before the
gates to Wawel Hill, which are open from 6am to dusk. For conservation
reasons a limited number of tickets is on sale each day. To ensure entry,
reserve timed tickets in advance for a moderate fee ☎ 012 422 1697 or
download a form from the website and email it to bot@wawel.org.pl

8 Smocza Jama

www.wawel.krakow.pl

Once there was a dragon, or Smok, who lived in a cave under Wawel Hill – and the rest of the story is the legend of Krakow's earliest beginnings.

You'll see images of a dragon everywhere in Krakow, recalling the story of the days when people first settled the land beside the Vistula River. It's said their king, Krak, built a castle on Wawel Hill, but was soon troubled by a dragon which terrified the people by seizing livestock and young women to take back to its den and eat. As kings so often did, Krak offered the hand of his daughter Wanda, and with her his kingdom, to anyone who could kill the evil beast. Knights came and went, each one dying without defeating the creature.

Eventually, a young shoemaker offered to try his luck. He put together a trap made from fat, sulphur and sheepskin, disguised as a fleecy ram, which he left outside the dragon's lair. At dawn the dragon awoke and swallowed the sheep bait for breakfast. As the sulphur burned in its stomach, the dragon drank deep in the river

to try to put out the fire, but he drank so much that he exploded. And the shoemaker, the princess and all the people lived happily ever after.

Today the dragon lives again, as a statue by Bronisław Chromy that breathes real flames. You can pay to climb down inside the dragon's den from the top of Wawel Hill, or just walk along the riverbank to see it.

➕ 120 F3 ✉ Wawel Hill ☎ 012 422 51 55, 012 422 61 21 🕐 Cave: Apr–Oct daily 10–5; Jul–Aug daily 10–6; closed Nov–Mar ✋ Inexpensive, under-7s free 🍴 Cafés on Wawel Hill (€)

Stara Synagoga

www.mhk.pl

This Renaissance building in the middle of Kazimierz is Poland's oldest surviving synagogue, now a museum of the rich Jewish heritage of the area.

The first synagogue on this site was built in 1407 and formed part of the Kazimierz city walls. The Florentine architect Matteo Gucci kept some of its brick-ribbed vaulting when he redesigned the structure in 1570. Other sections, used for women's prayer and administration of the community, were added later, in the 16th and 17th centuries. During World War II, Krakow's Nazi governor Hans Frank took the synagogue's chandeliers and turned the building into a warehouse. The vaulting collapsed and it remained in ruins until restoration into a museum began in the 1950s.

Today you can still see the synagogue's original late-Renaissance stone Ark, as well as a baroque alms box dating from 1638 inside the main entrance. The bimah in the main prayer hall, with a wrought-iron canopy over a 12-sided stone base, is a replica of the 16th-century original. Among the displays are a scroll with the text of the Torah, items used on

Jewish holidays, including plates for the Passover bread and kiddush cups used on the Sabbath, a menorah, photographs of the traditional religious life and a collection of drawings and paintings of the streets of old Kazimierz. Outside, a plaque in the pavement commemorates the spot where Tadeusz Kościuszko called Kazimierz to fight for Polish independence in 1794.

🔢 125 B5 ✉ 24 ul. Szeroka ☎ 012 422 0962, 012 431 05 45 🕐 Nov–Mar Mon 10–2, Wed–Thu, Sat–Sun 9–4, Fri 10–5; Apr–Oct Mon 10–2, Tue–Sun 9–5 🖐 Inexpensive, Mon free 🚌 Tram 3, 6, 9, 13, to Miodowa ❓ English audioguide inexpensive

10 Sukiennice

In the middle of the main market square, Krakow's Cloth Hall is still trading as it has done since the 13th century, though today it specializes in souvenirs not silks.

The medieval equivalent of a shopping mall, the Sukiennice is more than 100m (330yds) long and has always been at the heart of the commercial life of a city which grew on trade. The first Cloth Hall, built in the reign of Kazimierz the Great in the 14th century, was replaced after a fire in the 16th century by the current Renaissance building, decorated with gargoyles. Over the years, other market stalls and little shops grew up around it. The clear square you see today is the result of a 19th-century clean-up, when the female flower-sellers were the only stallholders outside the Sukiennice allowed to remain in the square.

Today you'll find stallholders in the Sukiennice selling jewellery in amber and silver, leather bags, sheepskins, linen, embroidered Polish folk costumes, stained-glass angels, decorated wooden boxes and carved wooden figures, as well as fluffy toy dragons and small knick-knacks for children. Look for the knife hanging on an entrance wall, said to be the one that the jealous builder of St Mary's Watchtower used to kill his brother, who built the Belltower.

The gallery of 19th-century Polish art featuring about 500 paintings and sculptures usually displayed on the upper floor has been moved to the Royal Castle at Niepołomice, while the restoration work continues.

🏛 120 D4 ✉ 1–3 Rynek Główny ☎ None 🛍 Souvenir stalls daily 10–8 💷 Free 🍴 Cafés in the arcades (€) ❓ The Sukiennice gallery will be at the Royal Castle at Niepołomice until at least 2010; daily 10–5 ☎ 012 261 9851; www.muzeum.niepolomice.pl 💷 Inexpensive 🚌 Minibuses leave from opposite the main post office in ul. Starowiślna

Exploring

The Old Town and Wawel   50–79

Kazimierz   80–91

Beyond the Planty   92–103

Krakow is a city with a strong, individual character. With an illustrious history as the the seat of archbishops and kings, it retained its personality even when, under partition, Poland ceased to exist for a couple of centuries.

The arts and architecture have always been important here. From the work of the Master Carver of Nuremburg, Veit Stoss, who made St Mary's altar, to the many Italian architects who created the city's baroque churches and palaces, to the contemporary violin virtuoso Nigel Kennedy, artists have chosen Krakow as their creative home.

Hand-in-hand goes academic life. From the time of the Krakow Academy, founded in 1364, to today's multitude of learning institutions, students energize the old place, and keep it buzzing. Even the Kazimierz, the former Jewish district, whose citizens were wiped out in wartime, is finding a new role, while celebrating its old one.

The Old Town and Wawel

At first glance, the Old Town appears to be a slice of living history – beautiful medieval, Renaissance and baroque buildings restored as designer hotels, traditional restaurants and cafés of great character.

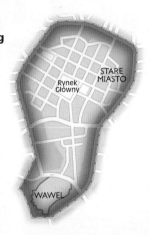

Yet underground, wild music and creative happenings stir in late-night cellar bars frequented by students, while on Wawel Hill, the castle and cathedral remind us this was once a capital city.

BARBAKAN

Krakow's 15th-century Barbican, one of the best-preserved
medieval fortifications you are likely to see anywhere, stands
on what was the most important trade route into the city and
protected the Royal Route to Wawel Hill. Originally part of the city
walls, today it stands alone, looking like a child's fort. You'll get
good views of the Planty and the city from the upper galleries,
and in summer (Jun–Sep) medieval pageants and knightly
combats are held here regularly.

www.mhk.pl

🚩 121 C5 ✉ ul. Basztowa ☎ 012 619 2320 🕓 15 Apr–Oct daily 10:30–6;
closed winter 🎫 The inexpensive ticket also gives entry to the city walls and
the Celestat Museum of the Marksmen's Guild

BRAMA FLORIAŃSKA

From 1300 onwards, future kings of Poland entered the city on
their way to be crowned at Wawel Cathedral through Florian's
Gate. The little that remains of the city walls stretches out either

THE OLD TOWN AND WAWEL

side of it. Here visitors can learn from a series of explanations in English how each guild of city tradesmen, such as haberdashers and carpenters, took control of one of the towers in the wall and defended the city from attack in times of need. These amateurs were trained by the Marksmen's Guild, still an important organization in the city today.

www.mhk.pl

🕂 121 C5 ✉ ul. Floriańska
☎ 012 619 2320 🕓 Gate always open; city walls, 15 Apr–Oct daily 10:30–6; closed winter ✋ Gate free, city walls inexpensive. Ticket also gives entry to the city walls and the Celestat Museum of the Marksmen's Guild

CASTLE WALLS

It can be difficult to tell which of the walls and towers that surround Wawel Hill are defensive and which are part of the fabric of the cathedral and castle. Farthest away, when looking from the Old Town, are the cathedral's baroque Clock Tower, Zygmunt Tower and Silver Bells Tower. From the east, you can see the Gothic Jordanka, the Danish Tower and Kurza Stopka or Hen's Foot Tower, with the baroque Zygmunt III Tower at the corner of the castle. The three tall brick towers nearer to the river are the Baszta Złodzieska or Thieves' Tower, Baszta Sandomierska or Sandomierz Tower, and the Senators' Tower or Lubranka. Star-shaped fortifications were added on the river side of the hill in the 18th century.

www.wawel.krakow.pl

🕂 120 F3 ✉ Wawel Hill ☎ 012 422 51 55 ✋ Free

COLLEGIUM IURIDICUM

Half-way down ul. Grodzka, a 17th-century doorway invites
exploration. Inside you'll find modern sculpture by Igor Mitoraj in
the colonnaded courtyard of a university building rebuilt several
times since its first incarnation as part of Queen Jadwiga's
bequest to the Krakow Academy, most recently in 1719. You can
visit the Jagiellonian University's Natural History Museum, across
the courtyard, which has thousands of marine shells, fossils and
butterflies, or in summer take in a concert in the courtyard itself.
✚ 120 E4 ✉ 56 ul. Grodzka ☎ 012 422 7711 ⏰ Courtyard: daily
7:45am–8pm; museum: Mon–Fri 10–6, Sat 10–3, Sun 11–3 ⛶ Free

COLLEGIUM MAIUS

Best places to see, ➤ 28–29.

COLLEGIUM NOVUM

Echoing in style the much older Collegium Maius, this imposing,
red-brick university building on the site of the 15th-century
Jerusalem and Philosophers' halls of residence dates from the
1880s. Sometimes you'll see groups of students and academics
gathered outside since all the university's ceremonies take place
in its Aula Magna, or Great Hall. If you are not graduating, your
best chance of seeing the interior is by attending a concert.
✚ 120 D3 ✉ 24 ul. Gołębia ⏰ Not open to tourists; view outside only from
the Planty, unless attending a concert

DOROŻKI

Krakow's cherished horse-drawn cabs, lined up near the flower
stalls day and night, winter and summer, are much celebrated
in poetry and legend. If you
decide to take a ride, pick
whichever one in the rank
takes your fancy; there's no
need to take the first, but
discuss the route with the
driver. You'll see the horses

are well cared-for – not only are they decorated with gorgeous trappings and tassels, they are shod with special rubber shoes to protect their hooves on the cobbled streets.

🕇 120 D4 ✉ Rynek Główny ☎ 012 431 2520; www.dorozki.krakow.pl is one company, office hours Mon–Fri 10–5 🕐 Daily early morning until the small hours ✋ Expensive–very expensive. The price depends on the length of the journey: the shortest is around the main square, about 70PLN, the longest is a round-trip to Wawel and Kazimierz, about 250PLN 🍴 Cafés nearby

JAMA MICHALIKA

In a city rich in café culture, this one stands out, although these days its allure is mainly historic. 'Michael's Den' was set up in 1895 and soon became a haunt of artists, bohemians and intellectuals, as well as the home of Zielony Balonik, the Green Balloon satirical cabaret. You'll see their art and cariacatures on the walls, and sit on the original art nouveau furniture.

www.jamamichalika.pl

✚ 121 C5 ✉ 45 ul. Floriańska ☎ 012 422 1561 🕐 Sun–Thu 9am–10pm Fri–Sat 9am–11pm 🍴 Café (€)

KAMIENICA HIPOLITÓW

Tucked away just off the Rynek Główny, this museum illustrates how life was lived in the grand houses of the Old Town between the 17th and 19th centuries. Its rooms are furnished for every member of the family, and the overall effect is rich and textured. Among the masses of ornaments and pictures, the little human touches – baby bootees or a child's homework – are engaging.

www.mhk.pl

✚ 120 D4 ✉ 3 Plac Mariacki ☎ 012 422 4219 🕐 May–Oct Wed–Sun 10–5:30; 2 Nov–30 Apr Wed, Fri, Sat, Sun 9–4, Thu 12–7. Closed Mon and Tue and 2nd Sun of month 👆 Inexpensive, free Wed all year 🍴 Magia café at entrance (€)

KATEDRA WAWELSKA

Best places to see, ➤ 32–33.

KOŚCIÓŁ ŚW. ANDRZEJA

St Andrew's stands out in a city almost completely built in Gothic and later styles. As the only church to survive when a Tatar invasion laid waste to the city in 1241, its 11th-century Romanesque lines look very plain compared with Krakow's more usual ecclesiastical extravagance, even though its two white towers later gained baroque cupolas. There's more baroque to see inside, with stuccowork by Baldassare Fontana.

✚ 120 E4 ✉ 56 ul. Grodzka 🕐 Daily 7:30–5 👆 Free 🍴 Café nearby

KOŚCIÓŁ ŚW. ANNY

Built at the end of the 17th century, the university church of St Anne's is a soaring example of high baroque, perhaps the best in a city which provides a lot of competition. Baldassare Fontana created the main altar, dedicated to św. Jan Kęnty, a professor and saint who was buried here in 1473, while the pulpit, supported by gold angels, and the gilded and painted cupola are other highlights among the dazzling riot of decoration.

www.kolegiata-anna.diecezja. krakow.pl

➕ 120 D3 ✉ 11 ul. św. Anny ☎ 012 422 5318 🕐 Daily 7am–9pm 🅿 Free 🍴 Cafés nearby

KOŚCIÓŁ ŚW. BARBARY

Situated next to St Mary's, St Barbara's church dates from the end of the 14th century and is said to have been built with the

bricks left over from the construction of its grand neighbour. Among the treasures inside are a crucifix on the high altar and a pietà, both dating from the 15th century. Restoration work has already enhanced the beautifully painted ceiling and is continuing.

➕ 120 D4 ✉ 8 Mały Rynek ☎ None ⏰ Daily according to the times of services; German Mass Sun 7pm 💷 Free 🍴 Many cafés nearby

KOŚCIÓŁ FRANCISZKANÓW

The Franciscan Church, rebuilt several times since it was founded in the 13th century, was almost destroyed in the great fire of 1850, giving the leading artists of the day a chance to raise it again. The cloisters still have murals in Gothic, Renaissance and baroque styles, but the main body of the church was painted with stylized Modernist flowers by Stanisław Wyspiański. He also designed the dramatic stained-glass window – God the Father – over the main entrance; at different times of the day it changes colour as the light strikes it. Look for Jósef Mehoffer's 1933 Stations of the Cross and the 16th-century Mater Dolorosa by Master Jerzy.

www.franciszkanska.pl

➕ 120 D4 ✉ 5 Plac Wszystkich Świętych ☎ 012 422 5376 ⏰ Daily 6am–7:45pm 💷 Free

CHRISTO TRANSFIGURATO

KOŚCIÓŁ ŚW. KRZYŻA

The Church of the Holy Cross is like a Gothic tree built in brick
– the ribbed vaulting of the interior is supported by a single
pillar in the centre. The church itself is well preserved, with
15th- to 17th-century wall paintings restored by Wyspiański,
a 15th-century font and a baroque altar and choirstalls.

✛ 121 C5 ✉ 23 ul. św. Krzyża ☎ 012 429 2056 🕐 Mon–Sat 7:30–6:30,
Sun 7:30am–9:30pm

KOŚCIÓŁ MARIACKI

Best places to see, ➤ 34–35.

KOŚCIÓŁ PIJARÓW

The 18th-century Piarist Church has an unusual rococo facade
added by Francesco Placidi about 30 years after the church
was built by Kasper Bażanka, who was not only a Rome-trained
architect but also became mayor of Krakow. The interior is a
colourful exuberance of trompe l'oeil painting by Franz Eckstein,
while the crypt, whose entrance is directly beneath the main
doors, is often used for concerts and exhibitions.

✛ 120 C4 ✉ 2 ul. Pijarska 🕐 Daily 7–7

KOŚCIÓŁ ŚW. PIOTRA I PAWŁA

SS Peter and Paul, the first completely baroque church in Poland,
was consecrated in 1635 and is distinctive because of the line of
statues of the Apostles which mark its frontage on ul. Grodzka
and which were erected to conceal the fact that the church
stands at an angle to the street. Inside, the baroque style is
continued in stuccowork by Falconi above the high altar showing
scenes from the lives of the saints, highly decorated tombs and
the organ loft. The Jesuit preacher Piotr Skarga, whose statue
stands on a pillar in Plac św. Marii Magdaleny, opposite the
church, is buried in the crypt. Look for the model of Foucault's
Pendulum, which demonstrates the rotation of the Earth.

✛ 120 E4 ✉ 54 ul. Grodzka 🕐 Daily 7–7, later for concerts; demonstration
of Foucault's Pendulum Thu 10, 11 and 12

KOŚCIÓŁ ŚW. WOJCIECHA

This little baroque church, sitting on Romanesque foundations, is one of the oldest buildings in Krakow. It is much used by locals who like to drop in for a quiet prayer away from the hubbub of the main market square. You can see everything inside from a seat in a rear pew, including the image of the church's patron saint, the missionary św. Wojciech, whose name is usually translated into English as St Adalbert. A small archaeology museum underneath the church shows finds from the church and square in summer when the weather is not too damp.

www.ma.krakow.pl

⊞ 120 D4 ✉ 3 Rynek Główny ☎ 012 422 7100; www.diecezja.pl ⏰ Daily 7–7. Museum: Jun–Sep daily 10–4, but often closed if wet ✋ Museum: inexpensive 🍴 Cafés in the square

KRZYŻ KATYŃSKI

The simple wooden cross standing outside the

14th-century Kościół św. Idziego (St Giles' Church) at the end of ul. Grodzka is a memorial to a tragedy in Poland's more recent history. It commemorates the murder in the Katyń forest in March 1940 of some 22,000 Polish officers, among them many academics, doctors and lawyers, by Russian troops acting on the orders of Stalin, who intended to wipe out the nation's leaders.

⊞ 120 E4 ✉ 1 ul. św. Idziego

MUZEUM ARCHEOLOGICZNE

While specializing in finds from Poland and its neighbours and concentrating on discoveries from the Malopolska region, the Archaeological Museum does not neglect world-class crowd-pleasers such as Egyptian mummies. Look for mammoth bones, 3rd-century BC golden treasure from the Ukraine, and Światowid, an early pagan idol resembling a stone totem pole, dredged up from a nearby stream. The garden bordering the Planty is a quiet place to relax on a summer's day.

www.ma.krakow.pl

✚ 120 E4 ✉ 3 ul. Senacka; enter from 3 ul. Poselska ☎ 012 422 7100
🕐 Jul–Aug Mon, Wed, Fri 9–2, Tue, Thu 2–6, Sun 10–2; Sep–Jun Mon–Wed 9–2, Thu 2–6, Fri, Sun 10–2 💷 Inexpensive, Sun permanent exhibition free; English audioguide inexpensive; garden inexpensive

MUZEUM DOM POD KRZYŻEM

The House under the Cross, a grand Renaissance building
previously used as a hospital and a monastery, has most recently
been a museum featuring an exhibition about the history of
theatre in Krakow. It is currently being renovated.
www.mhk.pl

➕ 121 D5 ✉ 21 ul. Szpitalna ☎ 012 422 6864 🕐 Currently closed

MUZEUM FARMACJE

Krakow's Pharmacy Museum is a surprisingly charming and
interesting place, with its world-class collection of examples
of the apothecary's art in a beautiful Renaissance building.
Highlights among its 22,000 exhibits are the alchemist's
laboratory in the cellar, complete with dried bats and crocodiles.

Faust is said to have studied at the Jagiellonian University, though it's not known whether it was here that he made his pact with the Devil. From here, up to the herbs drying in the attic, past the jars of leeches and pickled snakes, it's a fascinating archive of pills, potions and instruments.

www.uj.edu.pl

✚ 120 D4 ✉ 25 ul. Floriańska ☎ 012 421 9279 🕐 Tue 12–6:30, Wed–Sun 12–2:30 ✋ Inexpensive

MUZEUM KSIĄŻĄT CZARTORYSKICH

Best places to see, ➤ 36–37.

MUZEUM WYSPIAŃSKIEGO

The name of Stanisław Wyspiański crops up everywhere in Krakow. A painter, playwright, sculptor, designer and professor, he was born here in 1869, and by the time he died in 1907 he had made an indelible mark on every aspect of creativity in the city. His play *Wesele (The Wedding)*, is still much performed. His versatility is displayed in exhibits such as his model for a (never realized) 'Polish Acropolis' on Wawel Hill, paintings of the city and prominent characters of his day, designs for interiors, stained-glass windows and even a costume for the Lajkonik folk figure that is still in use. Several rooms are devoted to Feliks 'Manggha' Jasieński, the collector who introduced Wyspiański and other members of the Young Poland movement to Japanese art.

www.muzeum.krakow.pl

✚ 120 C4 ✉ 11 ul. Szczepańska ☎ 012 292 8183, 012 422 7021 🕐 May–Oct Wed–Sat 10–6, Sun 10–4; Nov–Apr Tue–Thu, Sat–Sun 10–3:30, Fri 10–6 ✋ Inexpensive; permanent exhibition free Sun May–Oct, Thu Nov–Apr 🍴 Café Pod Kasztanowcem (€), closed Mon–Tue ❓ Photography and filming moderate fee

PAŁAC BISKUPA EZRAMA CIOŁKA

Entry to the courtyard is free if you just want to admire the
medieval and Renaissance details of the architecture of this
palace in Krakow's oldest and best preserved street, but it's
worth venturing in to see the excellent collections of the Art
of Old Poland and the Orthodox Art of the Polish-Lithuanian
Republic. The first is composed of many coloured wooden figures
of saints and madonnas carved between the 14th and the 16th
centuries and discovered in churches in the region, while the
second comprises a priceless collection of 15th- and 16th-century

Carpathian icons, together with later icons showing Renaissance and baroque influences. Look for the 16th-century statue of Christ riding a donkey, the early 15th-century Madonna of Krużlowa and the Padovano angels. Next door, in the **Archdiocesan Museum,** is a reconstruction of the rooms at No 21 where Karol Wojtyła lived before he became Pope, while opposite at No 18 is the new John Paul II Centre (www.janpawel2.pl).

www.muzeum.krakow.pl

➕ 120 E4 ✉ 17 ul. Kanonicza

☎ 012 429 1558, 012 424 9370 🕐 May–Oct Tue–Sat 10–6, Sun 10–4; Nov–Apr Tue–Sun 10–6 ✋ Art of Old Poland gallery and Orthodox Art gallery each inexpensive; combined ticket moderate; both free Sun May–Oct; Thu Nov–Apr ❓ Photography fee moderate

Archdiocesan Museum

✉ 19 ul. Kanonicza ☎ 012 421 8963; www.muzeumkra.diecezja.pl

🕐 Tue–Fri 10–4, Sat–Sun 10–3 ✋ Inexpensive

PAŁAC BISKUPI

The bishops of Krakow have lived on this site since the 14th century, but this 17th-century building across the street from the Franciscan Church attracts attention today for its 'Pope's Window' over the main doorway. This is where the then Archbishop of Krakow, Karol Wojtyła, later to become Pope John Paul II, lived between 1963 and 1978. From this window he held his celebrated conversations with the students and faithful of the city.

➕ 120 D4 ✉ 3 ul. Franciszkańska

PAŁAC KRÓLEWSKI NA WAWELU

Best places to see, ➤ 40–41.

PAŁAC KRZYSZTOFORY

One of the grandest buildings on Krakow's main market square is the Krzysztofory Palace, named for St Christopher and built in the 17th century. In the past it gave hospitality to kings and revolutionaries; today different kinds of culture co-exist on different floors. The cellar club, where you'll find the latest urban music and modern theatre, spills over into the arcaded courtyard in summer, while the upstairs Fontana Room with its fine stucco ceilings is the venue for regular classical concerts. The palace is also the headquarters of the Historical Museum of the City of Krakow, with a permanent exhibition about the culture and history of the city. Every December, the palace continues the tradition of displaying the best *szopki* or Christmas cribs, made by local adults and children.

www.mhk.pl

🕂 120 D4 ✉ 35 Rynek Główny ☎ 012 619 2300 ⏰ Museum: May–Oct Wed–Sun 10–5:30; Nov–Apr Wed, Fri–Sun 9–4, Thu 10–5. Closed Mon, Tue and 2nd Sun of the month, 1 Jan, Easter Fri–Sun, 1 and 11 Nov, 24–25, 31 Dec 💷 Inexpensive 🍴 Courtyard café, cellar club (€)

PIWNICA POD BARANAMI

In the cellar of Dom Pod Baranami, at the far end of the main market square from the Krzysztofory Palace, the Piwnica Pod Baranami, or Alehouse Under the Sign of the Rams, was from 1956 home to Poland's most notorious cabaret. In its heyday, it was the scene of wild happenings devised on a shoestring and no one left until the early hours. Today, though the cabaret tradition continues on Saturday nights,

it operates as a slightly more sedate traditional
vaulted brick alehouse where the atmosphere
lends potency to the beer. The rest of the
building houses other arts venues including
one of Krakow's best cinemas.

www.piwnicapodbaranami.krakow.pl

🕂 120 D4 ✉ 27 Rynek Główny ☎ 012 421 2500
🕐 Weekly cabaret Sat 9pm–last customer leaves;
bar daily 11am–last customer leaves 💷 Inexpensive
🍴 Café/bar (€–€€) ❓ Book cabaret tickets in advance
Mon–Fri 11–3 at 26 ul. św. Tomasza or phone
above number

POMNIK ADAMA MICKIEWICZA

The statue of Adam Mickiewicz, Poland's most celebrated poet, has a prominent place in the Rynek Główny, though he never visited the city in his lifetime. Born in 1798, when the country was partitioned and had effectively ceased to exist, the writer of *Pan Tadeusz* was not only a Romantic poet, but also a political activist who wanted to see the resoration of the Polish nation.

He died in exile in 1855 while gathering a Polish legion to fight for his homeland and was buried in France, until his body was brought back to be interred in Wawel Cathedral. His memorial in the square, unveiled on the centenary of his birth, was taken down and sold for scrap during the Nazi occupation, but was recreated from original parts found in Hamburg after the war. It is a favourite meeting place of Cracovians, who have nicknamed him Adaś, and is garlanded on Christmas Eve by the flower girls of the Rynek Główny.

➕ 120 D4 ✉ Rynek Główny between Sukiennice and Szara Restaurant
🍴 Many cafés in the square

POMNIK KOPERNIKA

'Give me a place to stand and a lever and I will move the Earth,' said Archimedes, but Krakow Academy's most famous student, Nicholas Copernicus, went one better and moved the Sun. Until he published *On the Revolutions of the Heavenly Spheres*, it was generally believed that the Sun went round the Earth (rather than vice-versa). Although, being nervous of the church's reaction, he did not publish his revolutionary theory until he was almost on his deathbed in 1543, his ideas began to be formed during his studies here in his father's home town, between 1491 and 1495. You will find his statue in the Planty, near the Collegium Novum.

➕ 120 D3 ✉ ul. Gołębia/Planty

POMNIK KOŚCIUSZKIEGO

The mounted statue of Tadeusz Kościuszko takes up a commanding position on the slopes of Wawel Hill near the Coat of Arms Gate. He had a dramatic life as a main player in the politcs of his age on two continents. A soldier and engineer, he took part in the American War of Independence, fortifying Philadelphia and West Point and winning the friendship of Washington and Jefferson along the way. Returning to a partitioned Poland he led a continuing fight for independence, instigating the insurrection of 1794 in Krakow.

🚩 120 E4 ✉ Wawel Hill ☎ 012 422 51 55; www.wawel.krakow.pl
🍴 Cafés below the hill (€)

POMNIK PIOTRA SKRZYNECKA

The anarchic Piotr Skrzynecki, instigator and leading light of the cabaret at the Piwnica Pod Baranami (➤ 68–69), was central to the cultural life of Krakow up until his death in 1997. His statue, seated at a table outside the Vis-à-Vis bar, is always decorated with a fresh flower, in memory of his lively spirit.

🚩 120 D4 ✉ 29 Rynek Główny 🍴 Outside Vis-à-Vis bar

RESTAURACJA WIERZYNEK

Embodying Krakow's long tradition of hospitality in its many grand dining rooms, the Wierzynek Restaurant can trace its history back to 1364, when the prominent citizen Mikołaj

Wierzynek invited almost half the crowned heads of Europe and his own king, Kazimierz the Great, to a banquet. So well did the meal help defuse growing tensions in Europe that the king rewarded Wierzynek with a permit to entertain future important visitors to the city. Heads of state and celebrities (King Juan Carlos of Spain, the then American president George Bush and Steven Spielberg among them) have continued to come to enjoy the traditional Polish dishes – wild boar, roe deer and roast sturgeon with Polish crayfish are all on the menu.

🏛 120 D4 ✉ 15 Rynek Główny ☎ 012 424 9600; www.wierzynek.com.pl
🕐 Daily 11–11 🍴 Restaurant (€€€), café (€€), cellar bar and grill (€)

within the Planty

The medieval streets of the Old Town, lined with *kamienice* or grand houses, all circled by the leafy ring of the Planty, have remained unchanged since the city's charter in 1257.

Beginning at the Wieża Ratuszowa (➤ 79), walk past Kościół św. Wojciecha (➤ 62), and turn right down ul. Grodzka.

Ul. Grodzka is part of the Royal Route Poland's kings took to their coronations in the cathedral on Wawel Hill.

At Plac Wszystkich Świętych turn left into ul. Dominikańska, then left into ul. Stolarska. Crossing Mały Rynek, continue up ul. Szpitalna to Teatr im Juliusza Słowackiego (➤ 77), taking a detour right near the theatre if you wish to see Kościół św. Krzyża (➤ 61).

Branch out from the route at any point into the Planty.

Turn right along ul. Pijarska, passing Brama Floriańska (➤ 52–53) or walk through the Planty to the Barbakan (➤ 52), rejoining the route through St Florian's Gate.

Ul. Pijarksa borders the remaining part of the city wall.

Continue along ul. Pijarska. At the Czartoryski Museum (➤ 36–37) with its first-floor bridge to the Arsenal, turn left down ul. św. Jana. Turn right along ul. św. Tomasza.

At Plac św. Tomasza there is a little group of good restaurants where you can stop for lunch.

Cross Plac Szczepański and turn left into the Planty, passing Pałac Sztuki and its contemporary art cousin, Bunkier Sztuki. At ul. św. Anny, turn left and then right down ul. Jagiellońska past Collegium Maius (➤ 28–29).

Look into the courtyard at Collegium Maius to see the musical clock on the left-hand wall.

At ul. Gołębia turn right towards Collegium Novum (➤ 54), left at the statue of Copernicus (➤ 71) and wander through the Planty to ul. Podzamcze. Turn left.

Shortly, turn left up ul. Kanonicza, then cross Plac św. Marii Magdaleny and go left up ul. Grodzka back to the Rynek Główny.

Distance 3–4km (2–2.5 miles)
Time 3–4 hours
Start/end point Wieża Ratuszowa (Town Hall Tower) ✚ 120 D4
Lunch Café Camelot (€)

RYNEK GŁÓWNY

Europe's largest medieval square is little changed from when it was first laid out in 1320. The grand houses, or *kamienice*, on the square have been rebuilt after fires and according to fashion, Gothic giving way to Renaissance and baroque, as Italian architects became popular. Many are now shops and restaurants, so you can enter to see the remains of frescoes and vaulted ceilings. Several are still known by the emblems above their doors. 'Pod' means 'under the sign of' in Polish, so you can find Pod Obrazem (Under the Painting – an 18th-century Virgin Mary), Pod Białym Orłem (Under the White Eagle) and Pod Jaszczurami (Under the Fighting Lizards), as well as many others.

➕ 120 D4 ✉ Rynek Główny 🍴 Many cafés and restaurants (€–€€€)

SMOCZA JAMA

Best places to see, ➤ 42–43.

STARY TEATR

The Stary, or Old, Theatre was left in ruins after World War II, but has now regained its 1905 art nouveau brio. Originally converted from several older buildings in the 18th century, it had already been enlarged several times. From the outside, the frieze by Józef Gardecki is striking, while the interior features flower-painted ceilings and images of the great names of Polish theatre.

www.stary-teatr.krakow.pl

➕ 120 D4 ✉ 5 ul. Jagiellońska ☎ 012 422 4040 🕐 Theatre museum Tue–Sat 11–1 and from an hour before curtain-up 💵 Moderate 🍴 Café Maska (€) 🕐 Mon–Sat 9am–3am, Sun 11am–3am

TEATR IM JULIUSZA SŁOWACKIEGO

The Slowacki Theatre, with its swirling cream and white architecture, was modelled on the Paris Opera by Jan Zawiejski. As well as plays, opera and ballet, it hosts international touring companies, so you may find something to entertain you here.
www.slowacki.krakow.pl

✚ 121 C5 ✉ 1 Plac św. Ducha ☎ 012 424 4525 ◷ Box office: Mon 10–2, 2:30–6, Tue–Sat 9–2, 2:30–7, Sun 3–7 ✋ Moderate ⅌ Café (€)

WAWEL ZAGINIONY

Situated in the ruins of the Renaissance-era Royal Kitchens,
the Lost Wawel exhibition is an imaginative attempt to breathe
meaning into what's left of the Gothic royal castle and a
9th-century chapel. You can see displays of the different phases
of building on Wawel Hill and archaeological finds from all

over the hill which help explain its complicated history, as well as computer simulations of some of the buildings which are no longer there and a model of the hill in the 18th century.

www.wawel.krakow.pl

🕆 120 F4 ✉ 5 Wawel ☎ 012 422 51 55, ext 219 🕓 Apr–Oct Mon 9:30–1, Tue–Fri 9:30–5, Sat–Sun 11–6; Nov–Mar Tue–Sat 9:30–4, Sun 10–4; 1, 3 and 22 May, 15 Aug Sun hours apply; closed 1 Jan, Easter Sat–Sun, 1 and 11 Nov, 24–25 and 31 Dec 🖐 Inexpensive, free tickets on the day Mon Apr–Oct; on Sun Nov–Mar 🍴 Wawel Hill cafés (€) ❓ Last admission 1 hour before closing

WIEŻA RATUSZOWA

The Town Hall Tower is all that remains of Krakow's Town Hall, whose first incarnation appeared in the square in 1316. After a fire in 1820 and a general clearing of the square, the tower was left as you see it today. Climb to the top for good views over three sides – there are inexpensive telescopes you can use, so take some 1PLN coins. At the top you can also see the mechanism of the the former Town Hall clock. The current version is atomic.

🕆 120 D4 ✉ 1 Rynek Główny ☎ 012 619 2318 🕓 May–Oct daily 10:30–6; closed in winter 🖐 Inexpensive, buy tickets from Tourist Information Office on ground floor. Inexpensive photo permits extra 🍴 Café and theatre in cellar

Kazimierz

Less than two decades ago, Kazimierz was almost derelict – a sad, broken-down memorial to its former inhabitants, the thousands of Jews murdered by the Nazis.

Today, synagogues have been renovated as museums and cafés and restaurants serve Jewish food and resound nightly to the music of *klezmer* bands. For an alternative, go clubbing with Krakow's young bohemians.

STRADOM

KAZIMIERZ

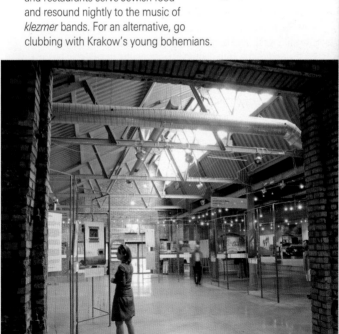

KOŚCIÓŁ BOŻEGO CIAŁA

The first parish church of Kazimierz the Great's new town, Corpus Christi Church was begun in 1342, but improved many times until by the end of the 16th century it became the vast Gothic basilica you see today. The highlight of the richly ornamented baroque interior added in the 17th and 18th centuries is a boat-shaped pulpit carried by dolphins and mermaids.

www.kanonicy.pl

✚ 124 B4 ✉ 26 ul. Bożego Ciała ☎ 012 430 6290; 012 430 6294 ☀ Daily, services 6:30am–7pm 👋 Free 🚋 Tram 6, 8 to Plac Wolnica

MUZEUM ETNOGRAFICZNE

This display, housed in Kazimierz's Renaissance old town hall, portrays the daily life and folklore of the people living in the countryside around Krakow, and is taken from some 80,000 items dating mainly from the 19th century. You'll find traditional Christmas cribs, examples of pagan festivals, beautifully embroidered Krakowianka folk dress and recreations of traditional flower-painted wooden houses, complete with butter churns and potter's wheels.

✚ 124 B4 ✉ Ratusz, 1 Plac Wolnica ☎ 012 430 5563, 012 430 5575; www.mek.krakow.pl ☀ Tue–Wed, Fri–Sat 11–7, Thu 11–9, Sun 11–3; closed Mon, 1 Jan, Easter Sat–Sun, 1, 3, 2 May, Corpus Christi, 15 Aug,

1, 11 Nov, 24–26 Dec  Inexpensive 🚌 502 to Plac Wolnica. Tram 3, 6, 8, 10, 40 to Plac Wolnica

MUZEUM INŻYNIERII MIEJSKIEJ

The Museum of Urban Engineering, situated in Krakow's former tram depot and bus garage, concentrates on vehicles manufactured in Poland and is a treat for lovers of old motor-bikes and cars. Children aged five to nine can pull levers, switches and ropes in the modern interactive science area. Although not all the explanations are in English, there is enough to enjoy on a short visit.

✚ 125 B5 ✉ 15 ul. św. Wawrzyńca ☎ 012 421 1242; www.mimk.com.pl 🕐 Jun–Sep Tue, Thu 10–6, Wed, Fri–Sun 10–4; Oct–May Tue–Sun 10–4 ✋ Inexpensive 🍴 Brasserie café/restaurant (€) 🚋 Tram 3, 13, 24 to ul. św. Wawrzyńca/ul. Starowiślna

NOWY CMENTARZ ŻYDOWSKI

Cross under the railway line on the far side of ul. Starowiślna to find the resting place of many of Krakow's eminent Jewish people, including rabbis, painters, professors and politicians. The New Jewish Cemetery was opened in 1800 when the Remuh cemetery closed because of lack of space. There's a memorial to those who died in the Holocaust to the right, just inside the entrance to the cemetery.

🕇 125 A5 ⊠ 55 ul. Miodowa ⏰ Sun–Fri 8–6; closed Sat, Jewish hols
🚌 Tram 3, 13, 24 to Miodowa ✋ Free ❓ Men to cover their heads to enter

PLAC NOWY

Though it's now at the heart of bohemian life in Krakow, and where many long nights of hedonism start, New Square today can seem rather quiet and faded. As 'Jewish Square' it was a busy place before the war, with a bustling market. The green Okrąglak in the middle, now used by fast-food stalls, was once a ritual slaughterhouse, and the square used to be the main trading place of the Jewish district. On one side of the square is ul. Estery, said to be named after Esther, Kazimierz the Great's Jewish mistress. Today there's a fruit and vegetable market most days, and a Sunday morning flea market, while the fast-food stalls offer huge, very inexpensive portions of *placki*, or potato cakes, and *zapiekanki*, a kind of Polish pizza on French bread, both with various toppings.

🕇 124 B4 ⊠ Plac Nowy ⏰ Daily. Stalls 8–4 🍴 Fast food daily 9am–2am (€)
🚌 Tram 6, 8, 10 to Miodowa

STARA SYNAGOGA

Best places to see, ➤ 44–45.

SYNAGOGA I CMENTARZ REMUH

The Remuh Synagogue, second in age to the Old Synagogue, is the only one in Krakow that regularly holds services. It was founded in 1553 by King Zygmunt August's banker Israel Isserles Auerbach, and named for his son Moses Isserles, a rabbi and Talmudic scholar, whose name was shortened to Remuh. Today no one ever sits where he prayed – a lighted lamp marks the spot. Despite wartime plundering, the synagogue's Renaissance collection box and late-Renaissance Ark survive, while the 17th-century bimah door comes from a synagogue outside Krakow. The rabbi is buried in the cemetery behind the synagogue. Closed to burials in 1800, this contains some of the oldest tombstones in Poland. During post-war restoration, some of the broken tombstones were erected alongside ul. Szeroka and now form Kazimierz's own 'Wailing Wall'.

www.krakow.jewish.org.pl

🔢 125 A5 ✉ 40 ul. Szeroka ☎ 012 429 5735, 012 430 5411 🕐 Sun–Fri 9–6; Sat 9–6 for prayer and services only 🖐 Inexpensive 🚌 Tram 3, 24 to Miodowa ❓ Female visitors should cover their shoulders, men their heads

SYNAGOGA IZAAKA

With a stucco cradle vault and Tuscan-style columns supporting the women's gallery, this baroque synagogue, built in 1644, is Kazimierz's largest. Legend tells us that Isaac Jakubowicz founded it after discovering treasure in his oven. Despite being despoiled in wartime, it still shows traces of 17th- and 18th-century wall paintings. Renovation is continuing.

124 B4 ⊠ 18 ul. Kupa ☎ 012 430 5577, 602 300 277 ⏰ Sun–Fri 9–7 ✋ Inexpensive 🚋 Tram 3, 13, 24 to Miodowa

SYNAGOGA TEMPEL

In contrast to the rather plain, white-walled restoration of Kazimierz's other synagogues, the interior of this progressive synagogue, built in the 1860s, is extremely colourful, with beautifully restored stained-glass windows and lots of gilt and Sephardic-influenced decoration. Britain's Prince Charles formally opened the Krakow Jewish Community Centre next door in April 2008.

www.krakow.jewish.org.pl

124 A4 ⊠ 23–24 ul. Miodowa ☎ 012 429 5411 ⏰ Sun–Fri 10–6; closed Sat and Jewish holidays ✋ Inexpensive 🚋 Tram 6, 8 to Miodowa ❓ Female visitors should cover their shoulders, men should cover their heads

a walk around Kazimierz

As you criss-cross the streets of the former ghetto, you'll pass fashionable bars as often as haunting reminders of pre-war Jewish life. Much restoration is going on and the area is changing fast.

With your back to the Old Synagogue, walk down ul. Szeroka towards the far end.

You will pass Remuh Synagogue (► 86) and the cemetery's 'Wailing Wall' on your left. Roughly opposite is the Popper Synagogue, now a youth centre. At the end on the right, Klezmer-Hois is where the ritual baths once stood. Gathered around this square are most of the Jewish-style restaurants in Kazimierz.

Taking the path by Klezmer-Hois, turn right down ul. Miodowa, cross ul. Starowiślna (watch out for trams), and carry straight on under the railway bridge to the New Jewish Cemetery (► 84) on your left. Retrace your steps, turning left on to ul. Starowiślna, cross and make your way down ul. Dajwór on your right.

The Galicia Jewish Museum (► 91) is active in keeping Jewish history and culture alive in Kazimierz.

At the end turn right on to ul. św. Wawrzyńca.

The Museum of Urban Engineering (➤ 83) is halfway down on your left. You could stop here for lunch or a snack at the Brasserie, which has a good reputation for its French food.

Cross back up ul. Wąska to ul. Józefa where you'll find the High Synagogue (➤ 90). Turn right up ul. Kupa to the Isaac Synagogue (➤ 87). Continue to the top of ul. Kupa.

You'll see the Kupa Synagogue, which dates back to the 1640s, on your right.

Walk back to the corner of ul. Miodowa and ul. Podbrzezie.

Here is the well-restored Tempel Synagogue (➤ 87).

Continue down ul. Miodowa away from the Kupa Synagogue and turn left down ul. Bożego Ciała.

The Corpus Christi Church (➤ 82) is a continuing reminder that at certain times Christians and Jewish people lived side by side in this area.

Leaving the church, turn right down ul. św. Wawrzyńca towards Plac Wolnica to the Ethnographic Museum (➤ 82–83).

Distance: 3.5km (2 miles)
Time: 2–3 hours
Start point The Old Synagogue ✚ 125 B5 🚋 Tram 3, 13, 24 to Miodowa
End point Plac Wolnica 🚋 Tram 6, 8 to Krakowska

SYNAGOGA WYSOKA

In the 16th century, when the High Synagogue was built, there were many ties between the Jewish people of Prague and Kazimierz, and this synagogue's design, much influenced by the style of those in Prague, is evidence of that. Called 'High' because the prayer hall is on the first floor, it originally had shops on the ground floor. Today it has a shop selling books on Jewish culture and music and CDs.

www.krakow.jewish.org.pl

➕ 125 B5 ✉ 38 ul. Józefa ☎ Bookshop: 012 430 6889 🕘 Daily 9–7 💷 Inexpensive 🚋 Tram 3, 13, 24 to Miodowa

ULICA SZEROKA

Though its name means 'Wide Street', Ulica Szeroka originated as the main square of the ancient village of Bawjół, and is said to be the first site of the Krakow Academy, later renamed the Jagiellonian University. This is where everyone gathers in June for the open-air closing concert of the annual Jewish Culture Festival (36 ul. Józefa, tel: 012 431 1517, 012 431 1535; www.jewishfestival.pl).

➕ 125 A5 ✉ ul. Szeroka 🍴 Many restaurants and cafés 🚌 Tram 3, 13, 24 to Miodowa

ZYDOWSKIEGO MUZEUM GALICJA

The highlight of the Galicia Jewish Museum is the exhibition Traces of Memory, which consists of photographs taken by the late British photographer Chris Schwarz, who was also the founder of this modern cultural centre. His pictures, taken over 12 years spent travelling around Poland with Professor

Jonathan Webber, who provides the commentary, document the remnants of eight centuries of Jewish life in Poland. The aim was to revive positive memories blotted out by the horror of the Holocaust. An inspiring and energetic man, Schwarz also set up a programme of events, including debates, other exhibitions, live concerts and talks, to keep the culture alive today and promote dialogue between faiths. His work continues.

➕ 125 B5 ✉ 18 ul. Dajwór ☎ 012 421 6842; www.galiciajewishmuseum.org 🕐 Summer 9–7, winter 10–6. Closed Yom Kippur and 25 Dec 💰 Inexpensive 🍴 Café (€) 🚌 3, 6, 8, 9, 13, 24 ul. Starowiślna/ul. św. Wawrzyńca ❓ Many special events. Contact the museum for details

Beyond the Planty

Outside the Planty, the circle of gardens and trees which replaced the old city walls, Krakow's residential districts of Kleparz, Stradom, Salwator and Podgórze also have a long history, interesting architecture and plenty of places of interest, while further afield you'll find green spaces, extensive woods and long views from mysterious mounds.

KLEPARZ

NOWY
ŚWIAT

Ogród
Botaniczny Uni
Jagiellońskiego

Park
W Bednarskiego

GRUNWALD

BŁONIA FIELDS

The vast Błonia meadow is a short walk from the Old Town, and is where Cracovians gather when the celebration or protest is too big for the Rynek Główny. As well as historic military parades and Poland's first football match in 1894, it was where Pope John Paul II said Mass and canonized new saints.

✚ 118 E4 ✉ Between al.3 Maja and ul. W. Reymonta 🚌 114, 164, 173, 179 to Cracovia Hotel. Tram 15, 18 to Cracovia Hotel

CENTRUM JAPOŃSKI MANGGHA

The Manggha Japanese Centre, a dramatic piece of modern architecture across the Vistula from Wawel Hill, was founded by the Polish film director Andrzej Wajda to display the Japanese art amassed by the influential collector Feliks 'Manggha' Jasieński.
www.manggha.krakow.pl

✚ 123 B7 ✉ 26 ul. Konopnickiej ☎ 012 267 2703 🕐 Tue–Sun 10–6
🍴 Restaurant (€) 🚌 Several to Jubilat/Most Dębnicki and Rondo Grunwaldzkie. Tram 1, 2, 6 to Jubilat/Most Dębnicki; 18, 19, 22 to Rondo Grunwaldzkie

DOM ŚLĄSKI

Best places to see, ➤ 30–31.

KOPIEC KOŚCIUSZKI

On a fine day you'll get an excellent view of the city and
countryside from the top of this recently restored mound. Poland
has a tradition of raising mounds, or *kopce*, to its heroes, and
Krakow has four. This one, dating from the 1820s, is a memorial
to the freedom fighter Tadeusz Kościuszko. You can find out
more about him in the museum in the fortifications below.
www.kopieckosciuszki.pl

✚ 118 E2 ✉ 1 al. Jerzego Waszyngtona ☎ 012 425 1116 🕓 Daily 9–dusk;
also evening opening with separate ticket daily May–Sep dusk–11pm;
museum daily 9:30–4:30 ✋ Inexpensive 🍴 Café with outside terrace (€)
🚌 Tram 1, 2, 6 to Salwator, then bus 100 from Salwator or 101 from Rondo
Grunwaldzkie ❓ Separate ticket for small waxwork museum

KOPIEC KRAKA I KOPIEC WANDY

Across the river from Kazimierz in the district of Podgórze is the mound dedicated to King Krak, legendary king of Krakow. Believed to date from pagan times and once topped with a mighty oak, it is near in age to Wanda's Mound in Nowa Huta, said to be the burial place of his daughter. Krak's Mound is sometimes called Rękawka, because of the belief that the people carried soil in their sleeves *(rękawy)* to build it. Rękawka is also the name of an ancient festival, which today lives on as a fair held on the Tuesday after Easter on top of Lasota Hill in Podgórze.

Krak's Mound 🕇 125 E6 ✉ Off ul. Lanckorońska 🚌 107, 139, 174, 184, 198. Tram 3, 6, 9, 13, 24, to Wielicka

Wanda's Mound 🕇 *125 C8 (off map)* ✉ Off ul. Ujastek 🚌 117, 138, 142, 149, 125, 132, 136, 139, 163, 172 to Sendzimir Steelworks. Tram 22, 23

KOŚCIÓŁ PAULINÓW NA SKAŁCE

It's said St Stanisław, the patron saint of Poland, now buried in Wawel Cathedral, was murdered on the steps of the Church on the Rock in 1079, apparently for displeasing the king. The church you see today is baroque, built in 1733. Outside is a statue of the saint overlooking the pool of holy water into which his severed finger fell. The crypt contains the tombs of eminent Poles such as the composer Karol Szymanowski, the artist Slanisław Wyspiański and the Nobel prize-winning poet Czesław Miłosz.
www.skalka.paulini.pl

🕀 124 B3 ✉ 15 ul. Skałeczna ☎ 012 421 7244
🕐 Church daily; crypt Apr–Oct Mon–Sat 9–12, 1–5,
Sun 10–12, 1–5; other times by appointment 🖐 Free
🚌 124, 128. Tram 6, 8, 10, 18, 19, 22

KOŚCIÓŁ ŚW. KATARZYNY

Founded by Kazimierz the Great in the 14th
century, St Catherine's Church has suffered
more than its fair share of disasters, including
two earthquakes. However, it still stands as
a good example of Krakow Gothic. There are
15th-century murals in the adjoining cloisters
and the church's good acoustics mean it is
often used for concerts.
www.parafia.augustianie.pl

🕀 124 B4 ✉ 7 ul. Augustiańska ☎ 012 430 6242
🕐 Daily, first service 6am, last 7pm 🖐 Free
🚌 124, 128. Tram 6, 8, 10, 18, 19, 22

LAS WOLSKI

In this forest, the biggest nature area in Krakow, is Piłsudski's Mound, raised in the 1930s in honour of Józef Piłsudski, general and politician. West of the city and stretching between ul. Królowej Jadwigi and the Vistula, it has eight walking routes, a winter ski route and a bike route. You will also find **Krakow Zoo** here, with a petting zoo, as well as snow leopards, jaguars, a herd of pygmy hippopotamuses and lots more.

✚ 122 B1 (off map) 🖐 Free 🚌 102, 134 (for the zoo), 152, 192

Krakow Zoo

✉ 14 ul. Kasy Oszczędności Miasta Krakowa ☎ 012 425 3551; www. zoo-krakow.pl ☎ Daily summer 9–7; spring/autumn 9–5; winter 9–3 🖐 Moderate

MUZEUM DOM MEHOFFERA

A real cradle of the Młoda Polska or Young Poland Modernist artistic movement, this house was the birthplace of Stanisław Wyspiański and home from 1930 of Modernist artist Józef Mehoffer, who entertained fellow artists here until he died in 1946. Mehoffer was a painter, printmaker, set and interior

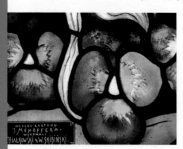

designer and rector of Krakow's Academy of Fine Arts, and he also created the stained-glass windows for Fribourg cathedral in Switzerland. He was also a keen collector, so this house gives an excellent impression of artistic life in Krakow between the wars.

✚ 119 D7 ✉ 26 ul. Krupnicza

☎ 012 421 1143, 012 423 2079; www.muzeum.krakow.pl 🕐 Tue, Thu 9–3:30, Wed, Fri 11–6, Sat–Sun 10–3:30 🍴 Ważka café 🕐 Daily 10–9

MUZEUM HISTORII FOTOGRAFII

Poland's only photography museum lies across the road from Dom Śląski (► 30–31). As well as a fascinating selection of

equipment dating back to the earliest days of the medium, including a magic lantern apparently illuminated by what looks like Aladdin's lamp, it has a permanent exhibition of intelligently arranged early snaps of the city and its citizens, portraits of historical figures, including members of the uprising of 1863–64, and a good programme of temporary exhibitions.

www.mhf.krakow.pl

➕ 119 B7 ✉ 16 ul. Józefitów ☎ 012 634 5932 ☎ Wed–Fri 11–6, Sat–Sun 10–3:30 🅿 Inexpensive 🚊 Tram 4, 14, 13, 24 to Plac Inwalidów

MUZEUM NARODOWE W KRAKOWIE

Best places to see, ➤ 38–39.

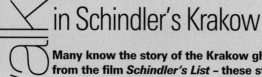

in Schindler's Krakow

Many know the story of the Krakow ghetto from the film *Schindler's List* – these streets in Podgórze are where the tragic events actually happened.

Walk over Most Powstańców Śląskich from Kazimierz or take a tram to Plac Bohaterów Getta. Cross the square diagonally to the small museum in Apteka Pod Orłem.

By 1941, there were only 20,000 or fewer Jewish people in Krakow, though they had made up a quarter of the population pre-war. Forced into just 320 buildings in a new ghetto in Podgórze, they began to die of hard labour, overcrowding and deportation to the death camps. Tadeusz Pankiewicz's Eagle Pharmacy, the only Christian business in the ghetto, was a centre of resistance and help. There's a map of the ghetto on the street outside the museum.

Retrace your steps to ul. Na Zjeździe, taking care crossing the main road to ul. Lwowska, and turn right.

After the junction with ul. Józefińska, you will see parts of the ghetto wall on the right, with a memorial plaque at Nos 25–29 ul. Lwowska. Fragments also remain on ul. Limanowskiego.

At ul. Limanowskiego, turn right and walk back up the main road past the square to ul. Kącik. Turn right and walk under the railway line to ul. Lipowa.

You'll see Oscar Schindler's enamel factory on the left at the end of the block of 4 ul. Lipowa. Though he was no textbook hero, he negotiated with the Nazis to release

Jews from the nearby labour camp at Płaszów to work for him and in so doing, rescued more than 1,000 Jewish men and women from certain death. Today the building is being converted into a cultural centre, but is not yet open to visitors.

Retrace your steps to Plac Bohaterów Getta.

The installation of overturned chairs in the square by Piotr Lewicki and Kazimierz Łatak symbolizes the scene after the liquidation of the ghetto on 13–14 March, 1943, when the remaining Jews were deported or murdered in the streets.

Distance 2 km (1.25 miles)
Time 30 mins without visiting the museum
Start/end point Plac Bohaterów Getta 🚩 125 C6 🚊 Tram 3, 24
Lunch Ogień restaurant at Qubus Hotel (€€) ✉ 6 ul. Nadwiślańska
☎ 012 374 5100; www.qubushotel.com 🕐 Daily 12–8
Apteka Pod Orłem
✉ 18 Plac Bohaterów Getta ☎ 012 656 5625; www.mhk.pl
🕐 Apr–Oct Mon 10–2, Tue–Sun 9:30–5; Nov–Mar Mon 10–2,
Tue–Thu, Sat 9–4, Fri 10–5 💲 Inexpensive, free Mon; audioguide
inexpensive 🚊 Tram 13, 24 to Plac Bohaterów Getta

OGRÓD BOTANICZNY UNI JAGIELLOŃSKIEGO

The Jagiellonian University's Botanical Gardens are Poland's oldest and largest, dating back to 1783. About 15 minutes' walk from the Rynek Główny, they are a relaxing place to visit, if not particularly grand or even very ornamental, with wooded areas, ponds and various display beds. One of the two greenhouse complexes is the Palmiarna, which houses a group of palms several storeys high – stairs bring you level with the top fronds. The other, the Viktoria, is named after the *Victoria cruziana*

Amazonian waterlilies that grow in its ponds, their leaves as big as coffee tables.

www.ogrod.uj.edu.pl

🏛 121 D7 ✉ 27 ul. Mikołaja Kopernika ☎ 012 663 3635 🕐 Daily 9–7 (9–5 winter months); glasshouses Tue–Sun 10–6; botanical museum Wed, Fri 10–2, Sat 11–3 ✋ Inexpensive

POMNIK GRUNWALDZKI

The striking monument north of the Barbican commemorates the Battle of Grunwald in 1410 – a date that looms large in Polish history. Showing King Władysław Jagiellon triumphing over the Teutonic Knights, it was commissioned by the composer, pianist and prime minister Ignacy Paderewski to mark the 500th anniversary of the victory. The original statue was destroyed by the Nazis but re-erected in 1975.

🏛 121 C5 ✉ Plac Jana Matejki 🚌 124, 152, 502. Tram 3–5, 7, 12, 13, 15, 19

STARY KLEPARZ RYNEK

If the splendidly restored main market square leaves you yearning for something more real, head north. Less than five minutes' walk away is the market at Stary Kleparz. It is typically Polish, with stalls selling pots, pans, garden seedlings, and lots of fruit and vegetables. You'll also find good local bread, cheese, sausages and honey, ideal for a picnic lunch.

🏛 120 B4 ✉ 22 ul. Krowoderska ☎ 012 634 1532 🕐 Mon–Sat 7–7

Excursions

Auschwitz-Birkenau	107–108
Częstochowa	109
Kopalnia Soli Wieliczka	110
Nowa Huta	111
Tyniec	112
Zakopane	112–113

For a change of scene, a visit to the medieval salt mines at Wieliczka takes barely half a day, and is much more fun than you might imagine. Another half-day and just a tram-ride away is the Socialist Realist suburb of Nowa Huta, whose steelworks have become the emblem of Soviet times. You can cycle to the monastery at Tyniec by following a pleasant riverside path along the Vistula, while at Częstochowa, you can see the country's greatest icon.

A visit to Auschwitz is not to be undertaken lightly, yet the camp will leave an impression that will last a lifetime. The mountain resort of Zakopane, by contrast, is a place of health and life, with green walks in summer, winter sports and a highland culture all its own.

AUSCHWITZ-BIRKENAU

The Nazi concentration camp whose name has become synonymous with the Holocaust is maintained as a memorial to the countless numbers who were murdered here in World War II. Many people feel obliged to visit, yet it's hardly an experience that fits easily into the average city break. Photographs are not allowed – remember the visitor standing next to you may have lost their whole family here.

The first slave labourers the Nazis brought to Auschwitz in 1940 were mainly Polish political prisoners. The terrible conditions soon killed many. Others died from starvation, criminal medical experiments or torture. Some were simply executed. By 1941 Soviet prisoners of war were being brought to the nearby camp at Birkenau, then, in 1942, the Nazis began bringing Jews from all over Europe for mass extermination.

After days travelling in rail cattle cars, they were unloaded and if deemed unfit to work immediately forced into 'shower rooms': the notorious gas chambers which killed 2,000 men, women and children at a time. It's thought that between 1.1 and 1.5 million died here by the time the camp was liberated in 1945.

You enter Auschwitz under the infamous gate with its slogan 'Arbeit Macht Frei' – 'work brings freedom'. In the blocks that once housed the prisoners, you can see photographs documenting their stories, possessions stripped from the dead – great heaps of human hair, shoes, spectacles, suitcases – and a film of the liberation of the camp. A

short journey away is Birkenau, where the wooden bunks would regularly collapse under the weight of the sheer numbers of skeletal prisoners crowded on each one, and where you can see the remains of the gas chambers and crematoria, as well as the railway line and unloading platform.

✉ 20 ul. Wiezniow Oświęcimia, Oświęcim ☎ 033 843 2022 (Mon–Fri 7–3); www.auschwitz.org.pl, www.um.oswiecim.pl 🕒 Site of the camp: daily Dec–Feb 8–3; Mar, Nov 8–4; Apr, Oct 8–5; May, Sep 8–6; Jun–Aug 8–7. Whole site closed 1 Jan, Easter Sunday, 25 Dec and for special events (posted on website) 🚻 Museum free; headphones, film, inexpensive; English-language guided tours of 3 hours 30 mins (book ahead) moderate; longer study tours available 🍴 Cafeteria (€) 🚌 Oświęcim train station, from

here there are several local buses to the Auschwitz site 🚉 Oświęcim ❓ Visits are not recommended for under-14s. Allow at least 90 mins for your visit. Most spend much longer. An hourly shuttle bus covers the 3km (2 miles) between Auschwitz 1 and Birkenau 15 Apr–31 Oct, or you can walk (about 35 mins) or take a taxi

CZĘSTOCHOWA

The reason everyone comes to
Częstochowa's **Jasna Góra monastery**
– pilgrim and tourist alike – is the Black
Madonna. This miracle-working icon
at the heart of Poland's holiest shrine
is unveiled daily with great ceremony.
Already hundreds of years old when
the Pauline monks brought her to their
monastery in 1382, she suffered scars
to her face in a 15th-century robbery
attempt. Two of the many times she is
said to have saved the country are when
the hill of Jasna Góra was besieged by
Swedes in 1655 and in the 1920 battle on

the Vistula against the Bolshevik Russians. Make sure you visit
the treasury museum and the other beautiful monastery buildings
and walls.

Częstochowa Information Centre

✉ 65 al. Najświętszej Maryi Panny ☎ 034 368 2250;
www.cestochowa.pl 🕓 Mon–Sat 9–5

Jasna Góra monastery

✉ 2 ul. O. A. Kordeckiego, Częstochowa ☎ 034 377 7777; www.jasnagora.
pl 🕓 Shrine daily 5am–9:30pm; holy icon uncovered at 6am, then covered
and uncovered at varying times during the day. Museums open daily summer
9–5; winter 9–4 💰 Expensive 🍴 Monastery café (€) 🚌 PKS coach station
45 al. Wolności, near train station and about 30 mins walk up al. Najświętszej
Maryi Panny or 11 or 18 local bus 🚆 Częstochowa Osobowa ❓ You need to
pre-book a tour to see the icon

Distance 140km (87 miles)

Journey time 2–3 hours by coach from Dworzec Autobusowy ☎ 034 379
1149; www.pks-czestochowa.pl; 90 mins–2 hours by train from Dworzec
Główny ☎ 034 366 4789; www.pkp.pl

KOPALNIA SOLI WIELICZKA

A tour of the salt mines at Wieliczka has become Poland's most popular visitor attraction. Serious mining of the valuable rock salt began here in the 11th century and hundreds of years of excavation have disclosed underground lakes and caverns so gigantic that today they house a cathedral, a ballroom and a concert hall, among other things. Salt miners down the ages seem to have inherited an artistic gene, too.

Your tour will take you past countless sculptures carved in salt. Much of the two-and-a-half-hour tour is an easy 2km (1.2-mile) walk below ground – the most difficult part is walking down 378 steps to the start. The deepest visitors go is 135m (443ft) below ground level, though the mine stretches down to 327m (1,072ft) and has about 3,000 chambers on nine levels. A lift brings you back to the surface.

✉ 10 ul. Daniłowicza, Wieliczka ☎ 012 278 7302, 012 278 7366; www.kopalnia.pl ◷ Apr–Oct daily 7:30–7:30; Nov–Mar daily 8–5; Easter Sat 7:30–1. Closed 1 Jan, Easter Sun, 1 Nov, 24–25, 31 Dec ✋ Expensive 🍴 Cafeteria above ground; simple restaurant at end of tour below ground (€) 🚌 Wieliczka Kopalnia, bus 304 from Galeria Krakowska; minibuses for Wieliczka Rynek from Krakow Poczta Główna (main post office) at junction of ul. Westerplatte and ul.Starowiślna, get off at junction of ul. Dembowskiego and ul. Daniłowicza in Wieliczka 🚆 Wieliczka Rynek, from Krakow main station ❓ Fee for taking pictures inexpensive

NOWA HUTA

This unlovely suburb of Krakow, begun on Stalin's orders in the 1940s, is today seen as a prime example of Socialist Realist architecture. The sights are very spread out so allow a lot of time (it's worth visiting the local museum first to get your bearings) or take one of the many tours from the city centre. Highlights are the Sendzimir steelworks and Our Lord's Ark, the Queen of Poland church, symbol of Polish resistance to Soviet rule.

✉ Museum of the History of Nowa Huta, 16 os. Słoneczne ☎ 012 425 9775; www.mhk.pl 🕙 May–Oct Tue–Sat, 2nd Sun of the month 9:30–4; Nov–Apr Tue, Thu–Sat, 2nd Sun of month 9–4, Wed 10–5. Closed every Mon, Tue after 2nd Sun, and every Sun but the 2nd Sun of the month 🚋 Museum inexpensive, Wed free 🚌 Tram 4 to Sendzimir steelworks, ul. Ujastek or 15 to Plac Centralny ❓ While you're out this way, drop in on the collection of 150 planes at the Polish Aviation Museum on your way back ✉ 39 ul. Jana Pawła II ☎ 012 642 8700, 012 642 4070; www.muzeumlotnictwa.pl 🕙 May–Oct Tue–Fri 9–5, Sat–Sun 10–4, Mon (open-air exhibition only) 9–4; Nov–Apr Mon–Fri 9–4 🚋 Inexpensive, Mon free 🚌 Tram 4, 15 to Muzeum Lotnictwa

TYNIEC

The Benedictine abbey of Tyniec, said to have been founded by Kazimierz the Restorer around 1,000 years ago, is about 12km (7.5 miles) from Krakow. It has a commanding position on a cliff overlooking the Vistula. Although it has had a chequered history and fires and battles have afflicted the church and the monastery down the ages, the 15th-century Gothic buildings and their baroque interiors are being restored and the religious community has been revived. A short trip here makes a pleasant drive or cycle ride out into the country.

✉ 37 ul. Benedyktyńska ☎ 012 688 5200; www.tyniec.benedyktyni.pl
🕐 Daily, with services 6:30–6:30 ✋ Free – donation suggested 🚌 112

ZAKOPANE

This mountain town, 100km (62 miles) from Krakow in the high Tatras, is Poland's winter capital and a destination in its own right. It has been a ski resort for more than a century, and today it has 50 ski-lifts and 160km (100 miles) of runs, including some that are world-class and several that are floodlit at night. It's possible to ski here until May, after which the hiking season begins. Walkers have 240km (150 miles) of marked trails to choose from in the Tatra National Park. The town's prosperity was kickstarted in the 1890s by the artist Stanisław Witkiewicz, whose **Willa Koliba** popularized the pretty, rustic 'Zakopane style' of wooden buildings, and the place has functioned as a retreat for Polish writers and painters ever since. On a short visit you can explore the craft shops along ul. Krupówski, sample the *góralski* cuisine and watch rugged, axe-wielding highlander folk dancers.

Willa Koliba

✉ 18 ul. Kościelska ☎ 018 201 3602; www.muzeumtatrzanskie.pl
🕐 Wed–Sat 9–5, Sun 9–3 💵 Inexpensive

Skiing and hiking trails: Tourist Information Centre ✉ 17 ul. Kościuszki
☎ 018 201 2211; www.zakopane.pl 🕐 Mon–Fri 8–6 🚆 2 hours 30 mins–
3 hours 30 mins from Dworzec Główny 🚌 2 or more hours from Dworzec
Autobusowy, depending on traffic; faster and more expensive minibuses
from the same bus station

Tatra National Park Office ✉ Tatrzański Park Narodowy, 42 ul.
Chałubińskiego, Rondo Kuznickie ☎ 018 206 3799, 018 202 3288;
www.tpn.zakopane.pl 🕐 Daily Jan–Mar 7–4; Apr–May 7–5; Jun–Sep 7–6;
Oct 7–4; Nov–Dec 7–3

Index

air travel and airports 18
Apteka Pod Orłem 101
Archdiocesan Museum 67
Auerbach, Israel Isserles
  86
Auschwitz-Birkenau 107–108

Barbakan 52, 74
Baszta Sandomierska 53
Baszta Złodzieska 53
Battle of Grunwald 102
Battle of Vienna 40
Bażanka, Kasper 61
beyond the Planty 93–103
Bielany 21
Błonia Fields 94
boat tours 21
Brama Floriańska 52–53, 74
buses 18, 19

Castle Walls 53
Chromy, Bronisław 43
Church on the Rock 96–97
climate 14
Collegium Iuridicum 54
Collegium Maius 28–29, 75
Collegium Novum 54, 75
Copernicus, Nicholas 29, 71
cycling 21
Czartoryska, Princess
  Izabella 36
Częstochowa 109

Danish Tower 53
disabilities, visitors with 21
Dom Śląski 30–31
dorożki 54–55
driving 14, 19, 20–21
Dworzec Główny 19

electric carts 21
electricity 23
embassies and consulates
  23
excursions 104–113
  Auschwitz-Birkenau
    107–108
  Częstochowa 109

Kopalnia Soli Wieliczka
  110
Nowa Huta 111
Tyniec 112
Zakopane 112–113

festivals and events 16–17
Florian's Gate 52–53, 74
Foucault's pendulum 61

Galicia Jewish Museum
  88, 91
Gardecki, Józef 76

health and safety 15, 23, 24
hejnał 34, 35
Hen's Foot Tower 53
Historical Museum of the
  City of Krakow 68
Holocaust 84, 91, 107, 108
horsedrawn cabs 21, 54–55
House Under the Cross 64

insurance 15
internet services 23

Jagiellonian University 91
Jakubowicz, Isaac 87
Jama Michalika 57
Jan III Sobieski, King 40
Jasieński, Feliks 'Manggha'
  65, 94
Jasna Góra monastery 109
Jerzy, Master 59
Jerzy, Prince Adam 36
Jewish Krakow 44–45,
  81–92
John Paul II, Pope 32–33,
  67, 94–95
Jordanka 53

Kamienica Hipolitów 57
kamienice 74, 76
Kantor, Tadeusz 39
Katedra Wawelska 32–33
Katyń forest 62
Kazimierz district 19, 20, 21,
  44–45, 50, 81–92

Kazimierz the Great, King 28,
  73, 82, 84, 97
Kazimierz the Restorer,
  King 112
Kęnty, Jan 58
Klezmer-Hois 88
Kopalnia Soli Wieliczka 110
Kopiec Kościuszki 95
Kopiec Kraka 96
Kopiec Wandy 96
Kościół św. Andrzeja 57
Kościół św. Anny 58
Kościół św. Barbary 58–59
Kościół Bożego Ciała 82, 89
Kościół Franciszkanów 59
Kościół św. Idziego 62
Kościół św. Katarzyny 97
Kościół św. Krzyża 61, 74
Kościół Mariacki 34–35
Kościół Paulinów na Skałce,
  96–97
Kościół Pijarów 61
Kościół św. Piotra i Pawła 61
Kościół św. Wojciecha
  62, 74
Kościuszko, Tadeusz 32,
  45, 72
Krakow Academy 91
Krakow Zoo 98
Krak's Mound 96
Krzyż Katyński 62
Kurza Stopka 53

language 25
Las Wolski 98
Leonardo da Vinci 36

Manggha Japanese Centre
  94
Marksmen's Guild 53
Matejko, Jan 39
Mehoffer, Józef 39, 59, 98
Michael's Den 57
Mickiewicz, Adam 32, 70–71
Miłosz, Czesław 96
Mitoraj, Igor 54
Mloda Polska (Young Poland
  movement) 98

money 22
Most Dębnicki 21
Most Grunwaldzki 21
Muzeum Archeologiczne 63
Muzeum Dom Mehoffera 98
Muzeum Dom pod Krzyżem 64
Muzeum Etnograficzne 82–83, 89
Muzeum Farmacje 64–65
Muzeum Historii Fotografii 98–99
Muzeum Książąt Czartoryskich 36–37, 74
Muzeum Inżynierii Miejskiej 83, 89
Muzeum Narodowe w Krakowie 38–39
Muzeum Wyspiańskiego 65

national holidays 16
Natural History Museum 54
Nowa Huta 96, 111
Nowy Cmentarz Żydowski 84, 88
Nowy Kleparz 18

Ogród Botaniczny Uni Jagiellońskiego 102
Old Synagogue 44–45
Old Theatre 76
Old Town 18, 19, 20, 21, 50–80
opening hours 24
Our Lord's Ark, Nowa Huta 111

Paderewski, Ignacy 102
Pałac Biskupa Ezrama Ciołka 66–67
Pałac Biskupi 67
Pałac Królewski na Wawelu 40–41
Pałac Krzysztofory 68
passports and visas 14
Piłsudski, Jozef 98
Piłsudski's Mound 98

Piwnica Pod Baranami 68–69, 72
Plac Nowy 84
the Planty 93
Pod Białym Orłem (Under the White Eagle) 76
Pod Jaszczurami (Under the Lizards) 76
Pod Obrazem (Under the Painting) 76
Podgórze 20, 93, 100–101
Pomnik Adama Mickiewicza 70–71
Pomnik Grunwaldzki 102
Pomnik Kopernika 71, 75
Pomnik Kościuszkiego 172
postal services 22–23

rail services 19
Rękawka 96
Restauracja Wierzynek 72–73
Royal Route 52, 74
Rynek Główny 21, 70, 71, 74, 75, 76

St Mary's Watchtower 34
SS Peter and Paul 61
Schindler, Oscar 100–101
Schwarz, Chris 91
Senators' Tower 53
Sendzimir steelworks, Nova Huta 111
Sikorski, Władysław 32
Silver Bells Tower 53
Skarga, Piotr 61
Skrzynecki, Piotr 72
Slowacki Theatre 74, 77
Smocza Jama 42–43
Stara Synagoga 44–45
Stary Kleparz Rynek 102
Stary Teatr 76
Stoss, Veit 29, 34, 50
Sukiennice 46–47
Synagoga i Cmentarz Remuh 86, 88
Synagoga Izaaka 87, 89
Synagoga Tempel 87, 89

Synagoga Wysoka 89, 90
Szymanowski, Karol 96

Tatra National Park 112–113
taxis 18, 20
Teatr im Juliusza Słowackiego 74, 77
telephones 23
time differences 15
tourist offices 15, 22,
tours 20
trams 19
Tyniec 21, 112

Ulica Szeroka 91

Wajda, Andrzej 29, 94
walks
around Kazimierz 88–89
in Schindler's Krakow 100–101
within the Planty 74–75
Wanda's Mound 96
Wawel Hill 74
Wawel Zaginiony 78–79
websites 15
Wierzynek, Mikołaj 72–73
Wieża Ratuszowa 74, 79
Willa Koliba 112, 113
Witkiewicz, Stanisław (Witkacy) 39, 112
Władysław Jagiellon, King 28, 102
Wojtyła, Karol 32–33, 67, 94
Wyspiański, Stanisław 39, 59, 61, 65, 98

Zakopane 112–113
Zawiejski, Jan 77
Zielony Balonik (Green Balloon) 57
Zygmunt bell 33
Zygmunt the Old, King 40
Zygmunt II August, King 40, 86
Zygmunt III Tower 53
Zygmunt Tower 33, 53

Acknowledgements

The Automobile Association would like to thank the following photographers, companies and picture libraries for their assistance in the preparation of this book.

Abbreviations for the picture credits are as follows – (t) top; (b) bottom; (c) centre; (l) left; (r) right; (AA) AA World Travel Library.

4l Tram, AA/A Mockford & N Bonetti; **4c** Chapel at Wawel Cathedral, AA/A Mockford & N Bonetti; **4r** Franciscan Church ceiling, AA/A Mockford & N Bonetti; **5l** Jasna Góra Monastery, AA/J Tims; **5c** Café Europejska, AA/A Mockford & N Bonetti; **5r** Wawel Castle Hens Claw Wing, AA/A Mockford & N Bonetti; **6/7** Royal Castle, AA/J Smith; **8/9** Flower Wall in Franciscan Church, AA/A Mockford & N Bonetti; **10/11** Jama Michalika Café stained-glass window, AA/A Mockford & N Bonetti; **12/13** Tram, AA/A Mockford & N Bonetti; **16** Grand Dragon Parade, AA/A Mockford & N Bonetti; **17** Parade of the Riflemen Fraternity, AA/A Mockford & N Bonetti; **20** Golf cart tours, AA/A Mockford & N Bonetti; **23** Telephone kiosk, AA/J Tims; **26/27** Chapel at Wawel Cathedral, AA/A Mockford & N Bonetti; **28** Cloisters at Collegium Maius, AA/A Mockford & N Bonetti; **28/29** Collegium Maius, AA/A Mockford & N Bonetti; **30/31t** Identity papers in Dom Śląski, AA/A Mockford & N Bonetti; **30/31b** Dom Śląski AA/A Mockford & N Bonetti; **31** Prisoners' needlework, Dom Śląski, AA/A Mockford & N Bonetti; **32** Wawel Cathedral High Altar, AA/A Mockford & N Bonetti; **32/33** Wawel Hill, AA/A Mockford & N Bonetti; **34/35** Mariacki Church ceiling, AA/A Mockford & N Bonetti; **35** St Adalbert's Church & Mariacki Church, AA/A Mockford & N Bonetti; **36/37** Chopin portrait in Princes Czartoryski Museum, AA/A Mockford & N Bonetti; **37** Meissen ceramics in Princes Czartoryski Museum, AA/A Mockford & N Bonetti; **38** Muzeum Narodowe w Krakowie, stained glass, Wyspiański and Mehoffer stained glass project, © National Museum in Krakow; **40/41t** Wawel Castle courtyard, AA/A Mockford & N Bonetti; **40/41b** Wawel Castle across river, AA/A Mockford & N Bonetti; **42** Souvenirs, AA/A Mockford & N Bonetti; **42/43** Dragon's Lair at Wawel Hill, AA/A Mockford & N Bonetti; **44/45** Old Synagogue, AA/A Mockford & N Bonetti; **45** Prayer Hall of Old Synagogue, AA/A Mockford & N Bonetti; **46** Knife in the Sukiennice, AA/A Mockford & N Bonetti; **46/47** The Sukiennice, AA/A Mockford & N Bonetti; **47** Rynek Główny at night, AA/A Mockford & N Bonetti; **48/49** Franciscan Church ceiling, AA/A Mockford & N Bonetti; **50** Margrave's House, AA/A Mockford & N Bonetti; **52** Barbican gateway, AA/A Mockford & N Bonetti; **53** Florian Gate, AA/A Mockford & N Bonetti; **54** Horse & tour guide AA/A Mockford & N Bonetti; **55** Collegium Novum, AA/A Mockford & N Bonetti; **56** St Andrew's Church, AA/A Mockford & N Bonetti; **58** Christ statue in St Barbara's Church, AA/A Mockford & N Bonetti; **58/59** St Anne's Church, AA/A Mockford & N Bonetti; **60** Piarist Church AA/A Mockford & N Bonetti; **62** Katyń Cross Memorial, AA/A Mockford & N Bonetti; **62/63** Archaeological Museum, AA/A Mockford & N Bonetti; **64** Pharmacy Museum, AA/A Mockford & N Bonetti; **65** Medical Society House detail, AA/A Mockford & N Bonetti; **66/67** Bishop Erazm Ciolek Palace, AA/A Mockford & N Bonetti; **67** Episcopal Palace, AA/A Mockford & N Bonetti; **68/69** Krzysztofory Palace, AA/A Mockford & N Bonetti; **69** Cellar Bar Piwnica pod Baranami, AA/A Mockford & N Bonetti; **70** Adam Mickiewicz statue in Rkynek Glowny, AA/A Mockford & N Bonetti; **71** Nicholas Copernicus statue at Collegium Novum, AA/A Mockford & N Bonetti; **72t** Kościuszko statue in Wawel Cathedral, AA/A Mockford & N Bonetti; **72b** Piotr Skrzynecki statue at Vis a Vis café, AA/A Mockford & N Bonetti; **72/73** Wierzynek Restaurant, AA/A Mockford & N Bonetti; **74** Grodzka Street, AA/A Mockford & N Bonetti; **75** The Planty, AA/A Mockford & N Bonetti; **76** Under the White Eagle, AA/A Mockford & N Bonetti; **76/77** Slowacki Theatre, AA/A Mockford & N Bonetti; **78** Town Hall Tower, AA/A Mockford & N Bonetti; **79t** Lion base of the Town Hall Tower, AA/A Mockford & N Bonetti; **79b** Lost Wawel exhibition building, AA/A Mockford & N Bonetti; **80** Plac Nowy peonies, AA/A Mockford & N Bonetti; **81** Galicia Jewish Museum, AA/A Mockford & N Bonetti; **82** Ethnographic Museum, AA/A Mockford & N Bonetti; **82/83** Corpus Christi Church, AA/A Mockford & N Bonetti; **84** New Jewish Cemetery, AA/A Mockford & N Bonetti; **84/85** Prayer Hall at Old Synagogue, AA/A Mockford & N Bonetti; **86** Wailing Wall at Remuh Cemetery, AA/A Mockford & N Bonetti; **87** Tempel Synagogue, AA/A Mockford & N Bonetti; **88/89** Tempel Synagogue stained-glass window, AA/A Mockford & N Bonetti; **90** High Synagogue, AA/A Mockford & N Bonetti; **90/91** Szeroka Street, AA/A Mockford & N Bonetti; **92** Mehoffer's House, AA/A Mockford & N Bonetti; **93** Grunwald Monument, AA/A Mockford & N Bonetti; **94/95** Kopiec Koscuizsko, AA/A Mockford & N Bonetti; **96/97** St Catherine's Church, AA/A Mockford & N Bonetti; **97** Church on the Rock, AA/A Mockford & N Bonetti; **98** Mehoffer's House stained glass, AA/A Mockford & N Bonetti; **99** Photography Museum, AA/A Mockford & N Bonetti; **101** Oscar Schindler's Telpod factory, AA/A Mockford & N Bonetti; **102** Botanic Gardens, AA/A Mockford & N Bonetti; **103** Grunwald Monument, AA/A Mockford & N Bonetti; **104/105** Jasna Gora Monastery, AA/J Tims; **107** Auschwitz II Birkenau SS Guardhouse, AA/J Tims; **108t** Auschwitz II Birkenau barbed wire, AA/J Tims; **108b** Auschwitz I exhibition, AA/J Tims; **109** Pope statue at Jasna Gora Monastery, AA/J Tims; **110** Miners sculpture at Wieliczka Salt Mine, AA/J Tims; **111** Our Lord's Ark, Nowa Huta, AA/A Mockford & N Bonetti; **112** Benedictine Abbey at Tyniec, AA/A Mockford & N Bonetti; **113** Farming in Zakopane, AA/J Tims.

Every effort has been made to trace the copyright holders, and we apologise in advance for any accidental errors. We would be happy to apply any corrections in the following edition of this publication.

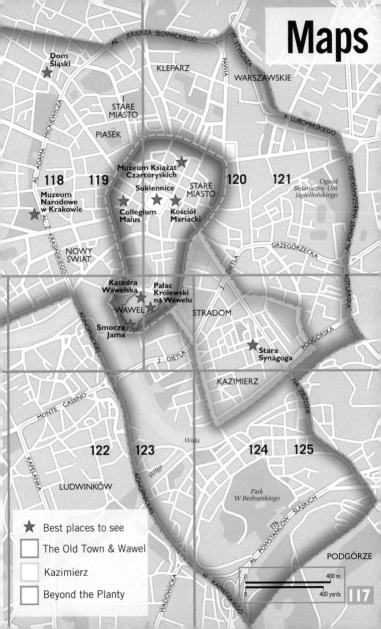

Maps

AL. JULIUSZA SŁOWACKIEGO
W. STWOSZA

Dom Śląski ★

KLEPARZ

PAWIA

WARSZAWSKIE

AL. ADAMA MICKIEWICZA

I STARE MIASTO

PIASEK

A. LUBOMIRSKIEGO

118   **119**

★ **Muzeum Książąt Czartoryskich**

Sukiennice ★

120   **121**

Ogród Botaniczny Uni Jagiellońskiego

Muzeum Narodowe w Krakowie ★

★ **Collegium Maius**

STARE MIASTO

★ **Kościół Mariacki**

AL. POWST WARSZAWSKIEGO

AL. Z. KRASIŃSKIEGO

NOWY ŚWIAT

GRZEGÓRZECKA

DIETLA

KOTLARSKA

Katedra Wawelska ★

Pałac Królewski na Wawelu ★

WAWEL ★

STRADOM

KONOPNICKIEJ

★ **Smocza Jama**

J. DIETLA

PODGÓRSKA

★ **Stara Synagoga**

MONTE CASSINO

122   **123**

KAZIMIERZ

NA ZJEŹDZIE

KAPELANKA

LUDWINKÓW

Wisła

Wilga

KONOPNICKIEJ

124   **125**

Park W Bednarskiego

H. KAMIEŃSKIEGO

WADOWICKA

776 AL. POWSTAŃCÓW ŚLĄSKICH

PODGÓRZE

0 ___ 400 m
0 ___ 400 yards

117

Legend

★ Best places to see

☐ The Old Town & Wawel

☐ Kazimierz

☐ Beyond the Planty

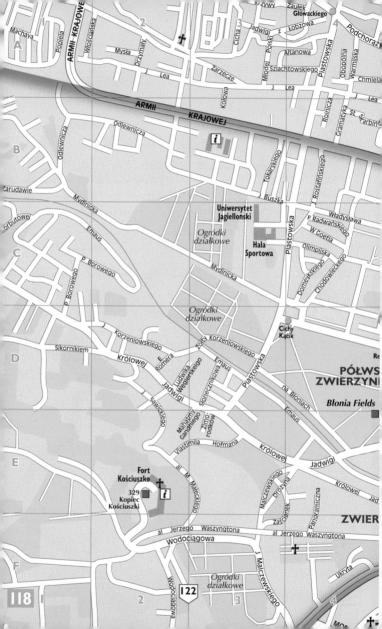

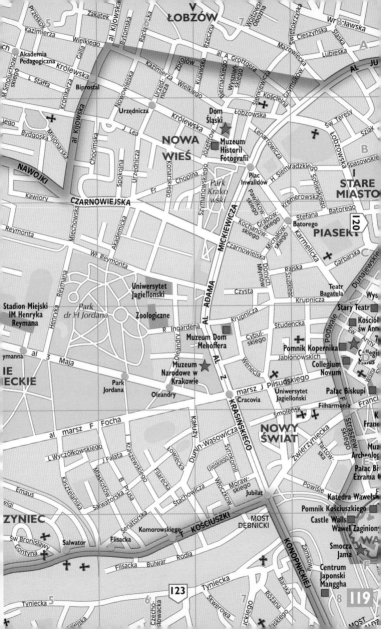

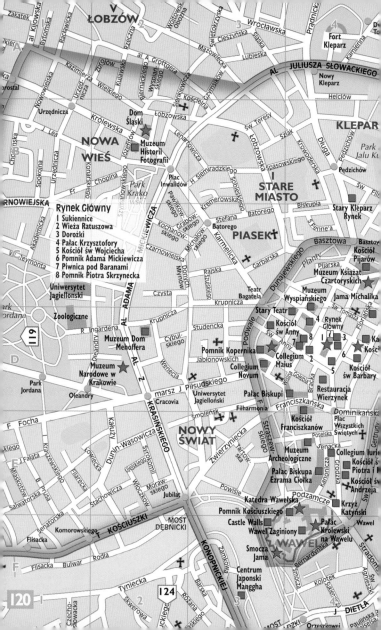

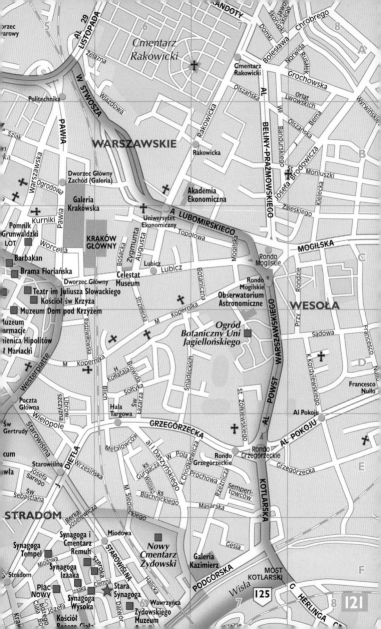

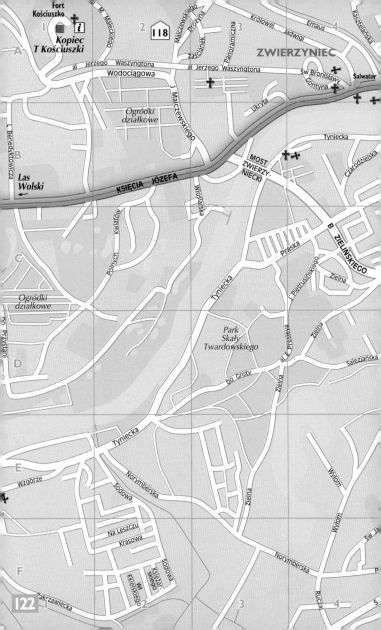

Fort
Kościuszko

**Kopiec
T Kościuszki**

118

ZWIERZYNIEC

Salwator

*Las
Wolski*

M Małeckiego

Malczewskiego
Drózyna

Panoramiczna

Królowej
Jadwigi

Emaus

Kasztelańska

al Jerzego Waszyngtona

al Jerzego Waszyngtona

Wodociągowa

Zaścianek

św Bronisławy
Contyna

L Benedyktowicza

*Ogródki
działkowe*

J Malczewskiego

Ukryta

Tyniecka

KSIĘCIA JÓZEFA

Wiślańska

MOST
ZWIERZY-
NIECKI

Czarodziejska

Pomnych

Kwiatów

Praska

B ZIELIŃSKIEGO

Zielna

Tyniecka

J Pietrusińskiego

Zielna

*Ogródki
działkowe*

Przystań

*Park
Skały
Twardowskiego*

al E Pręckiego

Zielna

Saleziańska

do Groty

Zielna

Tyniecka

Norymberska

Zielna

Wytom

Wzgórze

Sodowa

Wytom

Na Leszczu

Krasowa

Norymberska

Ruczaj

akrzawiecka

Sodowa
Księżarskiego

Wł Eklejskiego

św Jar

122

3

4

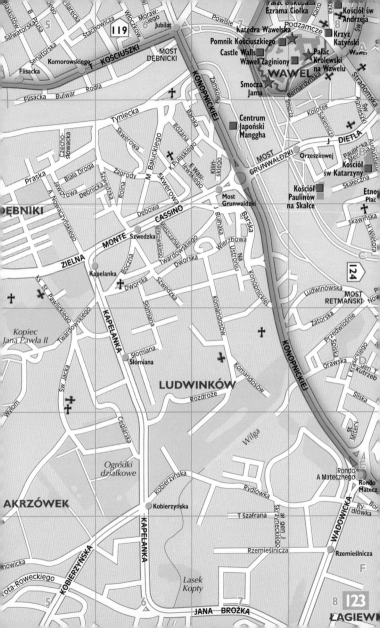

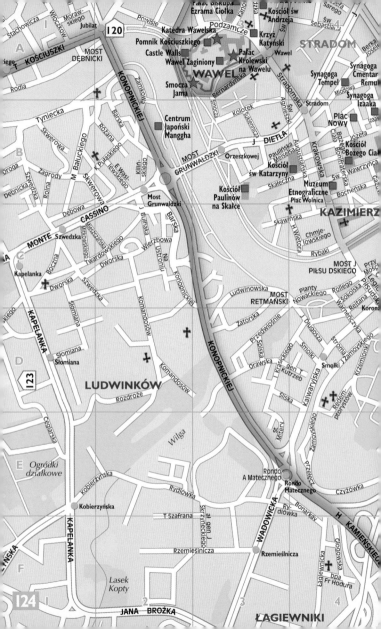

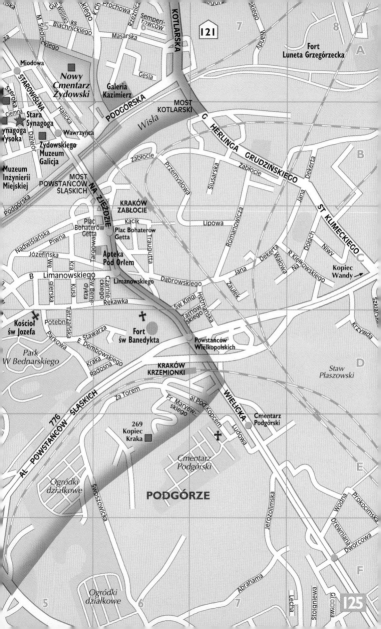

Gул Wkska ks
M. Siedleckiego Blachnickiego
za
Prochowa Rzeźnicza Semperi-t900...
Masarska
KOTLARSKA

121 7 8

Fort
Luneta Grzegórzecka
A

Miodowa
Nowy
Cmentarz
Żydowski
Galeria
Kazimierz
PODGÓRSKA
MOST
KOTLARSKI

G. HERLINGA GRUDZIŃSKIEGO

STAROWIŚLNA
szeroka
Ciemna
Stara
Synagoga
Wysoka
Halicka
Wisła

Dajwór
Żydowskiego
Muzeum
Galicja
Wawrzyńca

B

Muzeum
Inżynierii
Miejskiej
MOST
POWSTAŃCÓW
ŚLĄSKIEGO
Żabłocie
zabłocie
Podgórska
Przemyska
Ślusarska
Jana
Dekerta
ST. KLIMECKIEGO

Nadwiślańska
Piwna
Józefińska
KRAKÓW
ZABŁOCIE
Kącik
Plac
Bohaterów
Getta
Lipowa
Romanowicza
Dekerta Walowa
Doła
Niwy

NA ZJEŹDZIE
Plac
Bohaterów
Getta
Apteka
Pod Orłem
Traugutta
R Kiełkowskiego
Na Zjeżdzie

Limanowskiego
We
gierska
Kra
Kusa
Czarnie
ckiego
Limanowskiego
Dąbrowskiego
Jana
zaulek
C

Kopiec Wandy

Szklana
Krzywda

Kościół
św Józefa
Park
W Bednarskiego
Potebna
Potrzebna
W Benea
ckta
Rekawka
Św Kingi
Hermańska
Tarnow
skiego

atarzyńska
Parkowa
E Stawarza
E Dembowskiego
kraka
Radosna
Fort
św Benedykta
Fort
św Benedykta
Powstańców
Wielkopolskich
KRAKÓW
KRZEMIONKI
WIELICKA
Staw
Płaszowski
D

AL. POWSTAŃCÓW ŚLĄSKICH
776
Za Torem
Fr. Maryew-
skiego
al Pod Kopcem
269
Kopiec
Kraka
Cmentarz
Podgórski
Lipowa
Cmentarz
Podgórski
Wodna
Prokocimska

E

Ogródki
działkowe
Swoszowicka
PODGÓRZE
Jerozolimska
drewniana
Dworcowa

F

Ogródki
działkowe
Abrahama
Lecha
Stojałowskiego
gl cowa
5 6 7 125

Kluczbork
Krzepice
Olesno
Kłobuck
CZĘSTOCHOWA
Blachownia
Bory
Stobrawskie
A
Warta
Wyżyna
Krakow
OPOLE
Dobrodzień
Ozimek
Turawskie
Żarki
Koziegłowy
Myszków
Zawadzkie
Lubliniec
Kalety
Zawiercie
Strzelce
Opolskie
E40
Gogolin
Krapkowice
G. Św. Anny
B
Toszek
Siewierz
Ogrodzieniec
Tarnowskie
Góry
Zdzieszowice
Pyskowice
Ujazd
Wojkowice
78
DĄBROWA
GÓRNICZA
Piekary Śl
Będzin
Kędzierzyn-
koźle
Siemianowice Śl
Sławków
GLIWICE
SOSNOWIEC Olkusz
C
Kuźnia
Raciborska
Świętochłowice
Mysłowice
Knurów
Jaworzno
Trzebinia
Czerwionka-
Leszczyny
Mikołów
Chrzanów
Orzesze
Ledziny
Libiąż
Alwernia
Racibórz
TYCHY
A4
Kietrz
Rydułtowy
RYBNIK
Żory
Oświęcim
(Auschwitz)
Zator
Wodzisław Śl
Brzezinka
(Auschwitz-Birkenau)
Brzeszcze
D
Kravaře
JASTRZĘBIE
ZDR
Pszczyna
Wadowice
Hlučín
Bohumín
Goczałkowickie
Strumień
Czechowice-
dziedzice
Orlová
Karvina
Kęty
Andrychów
OSTRAVA
Petřvald
Haviřov
Skoczów
BIELSKO-
BIAŁA
Bílovec
Český Těšín
Cieszyn
1117
Klimczok
Żywiec
Sucha
Beskidzka
Fulnek
Bru Perk
Frýdekmístek
Ustroń
1252
Skrzyczne
1111
E
Odra
E462
Třinec
Wisła
934
Novy
Jičín
Příbor
Frýdlant n O
1220
Barania
Góra
Przeł Krowiarki
986
Fren Tát
Jablunkov
761
CZ
Vala Ské
Meziříčí
Rožnov
p Radho Těm
Beskid
Čadca
vod nadrž
Orava
Námestovo
57
30 km
Turzovka
1236
Wlk
Rácza
1226
Wlk
Rycerzowa
F
Vsetín
15 miles
1071
Krásno
n Kysucou
Trstená
922
Kysucké
Nove Mesto
SK
Tvrdo Ín
By ča
Žilina
Dolný Kubín
1709

126

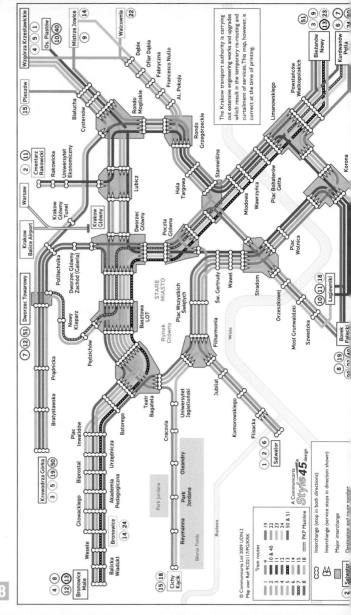

128